Living In The Real World

LIVING IN THE REAL WORLD

by Julie Crawford Taitt

Xulon Press

Xulon Press
2301 Lucien Way #415
Maitland, FL 32751
407.339.4217
www.xulonpress.com

Scripture quotations taken from the King James Version (KJV)—*public domain*.

Printed in the United States of America.

ISBN-13: 9781545615560

CONTENTS

INTRODUCTION

My people are destroyed for lack of knowledge: Because thou hast rejected knowledge, I will also reject thee, that thou shalt be no priest to me: seeing thou hast forgotten the law of thy God, I will also forget thy children. HOSEA 4:6

You may be reading this book because you are the curious type. You probably ordered this book or picked it up off a shelf or table because you are wondering what in the world could this title, *Living in the Real World*, mean? Perhaps you received this book from a relative, friend, or colleague who wanted to bless you by facilitating a change in your life for the better. However you made your way to this text, it is no accident. I believe the Lord wants to impart some wisdom, insight, joy, and hope to you today. Right now. Right where you are. Not only does the Lord want to do this for you, He wants to do it for your circle. This text is great to share with others as you journey through it. You will quickly see this as you review and answer the thought pro-voking, soul-searching questions at the end of each chapter. I believe the Holy Spirit will cause you to take stock, or as the Scriptures say, to *Selah* (which means to pause or rest and consider/ponder these things) at the end of each chapter and evaluate yourself. There is value in this reflection alone, and there is value in this reflection as part of a group. Let the Lord lead you down the path that will bring you the most growth. Let Him guide your footsteps in how to proceed with this material.

But journey on you must.

Everyone, everywhere, believes they are operating or living in the real world. Everyone who is alive today has no other choice but to live in this world – right? Our feet are planted on "terra firma." We think we know what is happening in the sphere around us. We have sources, both internal and external, which inform us about our world. We have various types of media—oral, written, social, you name it—that update us, as well as internal information, like instinct and intuition, that keep us apprised. We all want to believe we will know what to do in the face of various situations. We possess a range of emotions that enable us to deal with different circumstances. We have coping skills and defense mechanisms, which have been learned, honed, and fine-tuned from birth through adulthood. We understand how to handle our lives from day to day, because otherwise we perish. For the most part, we believe we are responsible, educated, smart, capable, resil-ient, flexible, and well adjusted. You may have even risen up the cor-porate ladder because of your own skills and abilities – or so you think. You are active and vibrant; you manage your business affairs with some level of assurance of success. You are able to make it from the beginning of the day to the end of the day. I know this is true because you are still here reading these words. Even when facing unexpected events--when life throws you a curve ball--you are able to put yourself back on the correct path. Right? You handle unscheduled, undesirable, or undeserved incidents by figuring a way around them. Don't you?

Perhaps you are reading this book because you want to unlock the keys to real living rather than just existing. You may have even asked yourself, "Isn't there more to life than what I am seeing right now?" You want to know what it really means to live in the real world. I was once like you. Notice I used the word *once*. It was not until I faced a trial that I could not see my way out of that the Lord God showed me that the only way through the situation I faced was to learn how to live and operate in the real world.

This is easier said than done.

This is why prayer and meditation on the Holy Bible, The Word of God, is so very vital and important to Christians. The Holy Bible was not written for God's use. It was inspired by God and written by men, for mankind. It was put in written form for our sake. It is during times of prayer and seeking after God that He will provide wisdom, insight, and answers to life's questions and issues. It is during those times of hard trials and difficulties that the Lord can show us and teach us what it means to *Live in the Real World*.

CHAPTER ONE

SEEING THE REAL WORLD

*J*ames 1: 5-6 states, "If any of you lack wisdom, let Him ask of God, that giveth to all men liberally, and upbraideth not; and it shall be given him. But let him ask in faith, nothing wavering; for he that wavereth is like a wave of the sea driven with the wind and tossed."

In the middle of my very difficult season, I asked the Lord exactly what He meant when He told me to live and operate in the real world. Wasn't I already doing this? Wasn't I already living in the real world? I mean, what other world is there than the real one in which I thought I had been living for many years? What have I been doing all these years while my feet have been walking on planet earth?

Now, in thinking about this issue of living in the real world, it is important that I explain to you that I am not the highly emotional type nor am I prone to fantasies and fairytale-like living. I would describe myself as a conservative, organized, structured, realistic, practical, disciplined (well . . . *fairly* disciplined), "Type A" person. If anyone knew what was real, I did. After analyzing myself, I surmised that this advice--this response--from the Lord must be for someone else. You know how we are sometimes: the Lord will show His wisdom for our lives and if it does not line up with our image of ourselves, we tend to overlook or modify it. Meanwhile, while I was analyzing and synthesizing God's direction for me, my situation continued to become more impossible.

God does not want us to be clueless about His guidance for us. Yes, the scriptures do say that we "see through a glass darkly," (1 Corinthians 13:12) and that "God's thoughts are higher than our thoughts and His ways are higher than our ways," (Isaiah 55:8-9), but I know that the job of the Holy Spirit is to bring us into all truth.

In other words, to make things known to us.

To shine a light on mysteries.

To give us clarity on the Word of God and His specific guidance for our lives.

The scriptures tell us if we sup with God will sup with us. Revelation 3:20 states, "Behold, I stand at the door and knock; if any man hear My voice and open the door I will come in to him and will sup with him, and he with Me." In other words, if we draw near to God, He will draw near to us. In today's words, He will pull up a chair and sit down with us. He will *hang out* with us. As stated previously in James 1:5-6, the scriptures remind us that if any man/woman lacks wisdom we should ask of God. God will not resent it; He will give it liberally. God's word lets us know that He wants us to have His wisdom and direction as we face life's situations. He does not want us to operate and live under our own abilities or strengths.

Instead, we can draw on His ability, His wisdom, and His strength. Proverbs 2:1-7 states:

"My son, if thou wilt receive my words, and hide my commandments with thee; so that thou incline thine ear unto wisdom, and apply thine heart to understanding;

Yea, if thou criest after knowledge and liftest up thy voice for understanding; if thou seekest her as silver, and searchest for her as for hid treasures; then shalt thou understand the fear of the Lord and find the knowledge of God.

For the Lord giveth wisdom; out of His mouth cometh knowledge and understanding. He layeth up sound wisdom for the righteous; He is a buckler to them that walk uprightly."

Just a few verses later, Proverbs goes on to say, "When wisdom entereth into thine heart and knowledge is pleasant unto thine soul discretion shall preserve thee, understanding shall keep thee" (Proberbs 2:10-11).

In other words, help and understanding are available to us for all of life's situations and challenges.

Isaiah 40: 27-31 states:

"Why sayest thou, O Jacob, and speakest, O Israel, My way is hid from the Lord and my judgement is passed over from my God? Hast thou not known? Have thou not heard that the everlasting God, the Lord, the Creator of the ends of the earth fainteth not, neither is weary? There is no searching of His understanding. He giveth power to the faint; and to them who have no might He increases strength. Even the youths shall faint and be weary, and the young men shall utterly fall: But they that wait upon the Lord; they shall mount up with wings as eagles; they will run and not be weary; and they will walk, and not faint."

Even though I did not particularly like or understand the instruction I received from the Lord on how to handle my situation, I nonetheless pondered it. I hope it doesn't impact your religiosity for me to say I did not *like* the Lord's instruction, or surprise you that I did not want to follow this directive. Let me tell you friends, the Lord already knew where I was. He is our Father, and Scripture assures us He knows our hearts.

He sees the heart.

He understands the heart.

There are no secrets from Him.

We do not deceive our heavenly Father; we only deceive ourselves. Our hearts and minds are known by God. It's easy for us to fool each other, to fool church leaders, to fool friends and relatives, and even to fool ourselves, but it is impossible to fool God. This issue is not discussed often in church, but I believe there are many people who are confused, resistant, and even angry about the guidance and instruction they are receiving from God in certain situations in their lives.

Getting in line with God's instruction required that I do some deep thinking, some meditation, and finally, that I take some action. Now whenever I am in a mode of deep pondering, I take a walk by a beautiful river near my home. It was while I was walking and praying that the Lord revealed to me exactly what it means to live and walk in the real world.

Man/Woman is a three-part being. We are made up of body, soul, and spirit. This makes sense because the Scriptures say we are created in the image of God and He is a triune God – Father, Son, and Holy Spirit. Genesis 1:26-27 explains, "And God said, 'Let us make man in Our image, after our likeness, and let them have dominion over the fish of the sea and over the fowl of the air, and over the cattle, and over all the earth, and over every creeping thing that creepeth on the earth.' So God created man in His own image, in the image of God created He him, male and female created He them."

The easy and popular way for us to live our lives is in the *soulish* realm--the area of our emotions. This is the area where we receive information based on our five senses – sight, hearing, smell, touch, and taste. When a difficult experience touches our lives, we often process our response to it based on what it looks like, what we hear about it, and ultimately how it *feels* to us. The problem with living based on an emotional reaction to a situation is that we can easily be deceived by the way things look or sound or feel.

Satan would have you believe that your circumstance is insurmountable, unconquerable, unchangeable . . . and maybe even eternal. He might even send someone else--a family member, friend, co-worker, or stranger--across your path to confirm for you how impossible your situation is. What I have come to share with you is this: although we may feel that we are living through an unmanageable situation, *it is not real*. I can say this with confidence because I know that each and every circumstance is very much subject to change – especially as we seek the power of God. The Bible declares that the only thing real in this world is what the Word of God says. Luke 21:33 states, "Heaven and earth shall pass away BUT MY WORDS SHALL NOT PASS AWAY" (emphasis mine). Isaiah 40:8 states, "The grass withereth, the flower fadeth; but the Word of God shall stand forever." These two scripture passages remind us that nothing is as permanent as the Word of the almighty God. Nothing is as real as the Word of almighty God. Nothing is as resilient; nothing is as resistant to change, as the Word of almighty God.

It is fixed.

It is settled.

Now and forevermore.

Your trials, your tribulations, your temptations, tests, and traumas are all subject to the Word of God. Yes, it is true that trials, tribulations, temptations, tests, and traumas can impact us and affect us. Yes, it is a fact that these things can produce stress and pressure in our lives. However, the good news is that trials, tribulations, temptations, tests, and traumas do not have the last word about what happens to you; the Word of God does. The Word of God has the last say and the final say. There is no greater authority, no greater power concerning your life and your situations. The Scriptures say that at the name of Jesus, every knee will bow, and that one day every tongue will confess that Jesus Is Lord (Philippians 2:10-11). Romans 14:11 reiterates, "For it is written, 'As I live,' saith the Lord, 'every knee shall bow to Me, and every tongue shall confess to God".

Your situation says you are disgraced and brokenhearted, but the Word of God says that He is the lifter of your head (Psalm 3:3). Jesus spoke in the synagogue at Nazareth about who He is and what He came to do for mankind, quoting Isaiah 61:1-3:

"The Spirit of the Lord God is upon me; because the Lord hath anointed me to preach good tidings unto the meek; He hath sent me to bind up the broken-hearted, to proclaim liberty to the captives, and the opening of the prison to them that are bound; to proclaim the acceptable year of the Lord, and the day of vengeance of our God; to comfort all that mourn; to appoint unto them that mourn in Zion, to give unto them beauty for ashes, the oil of joy for mourning, the garment of praise for the spirit of heaviness that they might be called trees of righteousness, the planting of the Lord, that He might be glorified."

Your situation says you are sick, but the Word of God says we are healed by what Jesus did for us on the cross. Specifically, Isaiah 53:4-5 states:

"Surely He hath bourne our griefs and carried our sorrows, yet we did esteem Him stricken, smitten of God and afflicted. But He was wounded for our transgressions,

He was bruised for our iniquities: the chastisement of our peace was upon Him; and with His stripes we are healed."

Not *would be* healed. Not *should be* healed. Not *could be* healed, *might be* healed, *may be* healed, or *will likely be* healed.

God's Word says we *are* healed.

Your situation says you are financially ruined, but the Word of God says He will provide for you. Philippians 4:19 states, "But my God shall supply all your need according to His riches in glory by Christ Jesus." Our Heavenly Father is rich in houses and land, and Romans 8:17 tells us that we are His heirs. Psalm 84:11 confirms, "For the Lord God is a sun and shield: the Lord will give grace and glory: no good thing will He withhold from them that walk uprightly."

Your situation says that enemies are rising against you and that you are defeated, but the Word of God says you are more than a conqueror through Him who loves you. Romans 8:31*b* states, "If God is for us, who is against us?" Proverb 30:5 states, "Every word of God is pure: He is a shield unto them that put their trust in Him." There is no plot, no plan, no trick, no trap, no wisdom, no ploy, no insight, no strategy the enemy has planned against you that can overtake the shield the Lord has erected to protect you. Another way to state this is found in Proverbs 21:30- 31, (paraphrased): Regardless of what wicked plan the enemy has for our lives, no matter what horse he makes ready to battle against us or what weapons he lines up; no matter what support he gathers or what reinforcements he calls; no matter what team he recruits against us, we can be sure that victory rests with the Lord.

Safety rests with the Lord.

Success rests with the Lord.

Security rests with the Lord.

His shield will not fail. Having walked through many spiritual battles in my life, I am a living witness that this is true. I am not just talking about something I have heard; I have lived this. This is my confession.

There have been times when I have had to remind myself of this truth in Romans 8:32-37 (paraphrased), even through my own tears:

> He who did not spare His own Son, but delivered Him over for us all, how will He not also with Him freely give us all things? Who will bring a charge against God's elect? God is the one who justifies; who is the one who condemns? Christ Jesus is He who died, yes, rather who was raised, who sits at the right hand of God who also intercedes for us. Who will separate us from the love of Christ? Will tribulation, or distress, or persecution, or famine, or nakedness, or peril or sword? Just as it is written, "For your sake we are being put to death all day long; we were considered as sheep to be slaughtered." But in all these things we

overwhelmingly conquer through Him who loved us.

Romans 8:38-39 sums up, "For I am persuaded that neither death, nor life, nor angels, nor principalities, nor powers, nor things present, nor things to come, nor height, nor depth, nor any other creature shall be able to separate us from the love of God, which is in Christ Jesus our Lord."

The Word of God says that when your enemies come in to eat your flesh they will fail: "When the wicked, even mine enemies and my foes, came upon me to eat up my flesh, they stumbled and fell" (Psalm 27:2). Deuteronomy 28:7 says that your enemies may come in one way, but they will flee seven ways. Psalm 44: 5-8 assures,

> "Through Thee (God) we will push down our enemies: through Thy name will we tread them under that rise up against us. For I will not trust in my bow, neither shall my sword save me, but Thou hast saved us from our enemies, and hast put them to shame that hated us. In God

we boast all the day long and praise Thy name forever."

Your situation says you are required to do something you may not feel equipped to accomplish, but the Word of God promises, "You can do all things through Christ who strengtheneth you" (Philippians 4:13).

Your situation says you are a "loser" but the Word of God says you are a winner through Jesus Christ in every situation. 1 Corinthians 15:57 states, "But thanks be to God, which giveth us the victory through our Lord Jesus Christ."

Your situation says that you are alone and that you aren't going to make it, but the Scripture states: "God is our refuge and strength, a very present help in trouble. Therefore will not we fear, though the earth be removed, and though the mountains be carried into the midst of the sea. Though the waters thereof roar and be troubled, though the mountains shake with the swelling thereof" (Psalm 46:1-3). In times of trouble and doubt, God assures us that He is right there with us--an ever-present, willing, and able helper in our times of trouble.

Your situation says that you will never find joy, but the Word of the Lord says that there is joy in the Lord and that His joy is your strength. Nehemiah 8:10 states, "Then he said unto them, "Go your way, eat the fat, and drink the sweet, and send portions unto them for whom nothing is prepared: for this day is holy unto our Lord: neither be ye sorry; for the joy of the Lord is your strength."

Your situation is not as real as the Word of God is. Your circumstances are not as real as what God's Word says about you. The spiritual realm is much more real than this natural world in which we live. The condition of your life is subject to be changed instantly but God is constant and consistent, unchanging and unwavering. Malachi 3:6 states, "For I am the Lord and I change not." Hebrews 13:8 reiterates, "Jesus Christ is the same yesterday and today and forever." Numbers 23:19 assures us, "God is not a man, that He should lie, nor a son of man, that He should repent; Hath He said, and shall He not do it? Or hath

He spoken, and shall He not make it good?" He does not change. His Word does not change. His promises are true. This is what's real.

When we dissect the word *circumstances,* we see that *circum* is the same root for our word *circumference*, meaning round or circular. In Merriam-Webster's Collegiate Dictionary (Tenth Edition) the word *circum* means "around." The same Dictionary defines the word *stance* as "position, posture, stay, a way of standing or being placed". Thus, your trials and tribulations--your circumstances--are simply the situations standing around you. You need to speak God's word to them so that they will stop standing around you and find something other to do than afflict you. One suggestion is to tell them to be cast into the sea. Jesus said in Matthew 17:20, "If ye have faith as a grain of mustard seed, you shall say unto this mountain, 'Remove hence to yonder place;" and it shall remove; and nothing shall be impossible unto you."

Instead of repeating what my five senses were telling me about my dilemma, I began to apply God's Word to my situation by repeating what

His Word says about me as a believer, as a born-again child of God. I began to live like God's Word was more real than my circumstances. I began to walk like a joint heir with Christ Jesus. I won't tell you it was a "bed of roses" to think and live this way at first. But what happened immediately was that God began to boost my faith and my level of expectation.

This was a big deal. This was great improvement. My problem had worked so intensely on my emotions and thoughts that at one point I had become angry with God. I accused – Him of abandoning me. I accused Him of not being there to handle the really hard stuff in my life. I had begun to believe that God was busy somewhere else--probably helping some little old lady get a parking spot on her weekly trip to the market--while I needed some *real* help.

I had done all I knew to do.

I had come to the end of my rope--the end of my own skills, abilities and talents.

I had run out of steam.

I was going down under the water for the third time when the Lord threw me a lifeline. He instructed me to look beyond what I was seeing with my own, natural eyes. These problems of mine were not more real—not even *as* real--as God's promises in His Word. God's arms were not too short to reach down and touch my situation.

This is what I learned: Be led by your spirit, and not by your emotions and fleshly desires. Do what the Spirit of God says in your circumstance, not what worldly advice says. Operate in the real world, which actually *is* the *spiritual realm*. Let the Holy Spirit have dominion in your life. You are not a victim, but a victor. You are not a wimp, but a warrior. Deuteronomy 20:18 says you are the head and not the tail.

You are not a loser.

You are a winner.

The end is not here; the best is still yet to come. You are not alone, for Deuteronomy 31:6-8 promises that God is with you. Hebrews 13:5 says that God will never desert you, nor will He ever forsake you. You are not unprotected, as Psalm 91:11-13 states, "For He will give His angels charge concerning you, to guard you in your ways. They will bear you up in their hands, that you do not strike your foot against a stone. You will tread upon and trample down the lion and cobra, the young lion and the serpent." The Psalm goes on to proclaim in verses 14-16 that because we have loved God, He will deliver us. That God will set us securely on high because we know His name; that when we call upon the Lord, He will answer us.

That He will be with us in trouble.

That He will rescue us and honor us.

That He will satisfy us with a long life.

That we will see His salvation."

God is real. Faith is a lot stronger than what you feel. Feelings are deceptive and are subject to quickly change. The only solid foundation is the Word of God. Continue to read God's Word and learn how to live and operate in the real world in your own circumstances, dilemmas, difficulties, challenges, trials, traumas, and tribulations.

STUDY AND DISCUSSION QUESTIONS - CHAPTER ONE

1. Reflect upon a situation in your life in which you faced a problem and felt there was no solution.

2. Describe your feelings surrounding this situation at the time. Describe your feelings about it now.

3. What was the answer the Lord gave you about how to handle it?

4. What do you believe were the lessons the Lord had for you in that experience?

5. What does Living and Operating in the Real World mean for you?

6. When you think of other people in your life, what do you see in their actions or words that demonstrate whether they are living and operating in the real world?

7. Describe some strategies you have utilized to help yourself and others learn to live and operate in the real world.

8. Take a few minutes now and write a short prayer of gratitude to the Lord for bringing you through and helping you to be stronger. If you are presently in the middle of a challenging situation, pray for the Lord to show you how to live and operate in the real world right now in the midst of it.

CHAPTER TWO

OPERATING IN THE LOVE WORLD

*S*everal years ago, the Lord had me repeatedly read 1 Corinthians 13. I read it on the bus every morning on my way to work. I read it every day at lunchtime. I read it at night before going to bed. I was reading it for my daily devotional time. I just could not seem to move past this scripture or read anything else for several months. While I enjoyed reading it, I also felt a deep pull, a connection to this particular passage of Scripture. This passage is frequently referred to as the "Love" chapter. It is believed by biblical scholars to have been written by Paul to the people in the city of Corinth, to instruct them on how vitally important it was for them to love. In 1 Corinthians 12, Paul talks to the people of Corinth about Spiritual Gifts and their utilization. In 1 Corinthians 13, he informs and reminds the people of Corinth that while Spiritual Gifts are important, they have no real value or impact if they are not coupled with love. In Chapter 13, Paul defines "real love." He does not want his audience to be ineffective in their spiritual lives due to lack of love for others. Great faith, great service, and great works are meaningless if they are not motivated by and connected with genuine love. At the time I was reading this "Love Chapter," I had no idea how much I would need to remember the truths it contained.

Years later, after having immersed myself in this chapter about love and what it really means to love, I became an ordained minister and began working with all kinds of people. I ministered to Christians and non-Christians, to the saved and the unsaved, to the nice, the not-so-nice, the untouchables, the good, the bad, and the ugly. It was then that I realized why I needed to read this chapter both day and night. Oh don't get me wrong, I love the work of the ministry, but it certainly gives many opportunities to practice what you preach. The Scripture states in Galatians 5:22-23, "But the fruit of the spirit is love, joy, peace, longsuffering, gentleness, goodness, faith, meekness, and temperance; against such there is no law," but there were days when my fruit of the Spirit (love, joy, peace, longsuffering, gentleness, goodness, faith, meekness, and temperance) began to feel like they were fully ripened and just about ready to fall off the tree! I really began to ponder this fruit of the spirit, and I realized they are all interconnected; they all build upon each other.

For example, it is almost impossible to have temperance (self-control) if you are not willing to be patient, longsuffering, and faithful. Having poor impulse control, over-reacting, and speaking before you think are all evidence of a lack of self-control. Webster's 1913 dictionary defines *self-control* as "Control of one's self; restraint exercised over one's self, self command." The Word Net Dictionary defines *self-control* as "the act of denying oneself, controlling one's impulses, self-denial, self-discipline, the trait of resolutely controlling one's own behavior, self-possession, willpower, self-will." Patience will allow you to wait out a situation and maintain self control because you have the faith that God is working it out and that you can trust Him. Patience will give you the assurance that you do not have to fight every battle. 1 Samuel 17:47 tells us that the battle is not ours, but rather it is the Lord's to fight on our behalf. There have been many occasions in my life in which I have regretted not having patience in a situation. In most of those situations I ultimately saw God work things out, but I later realized that I frustrated my own path by my lack of patience.

Having love for God and others will cause you to be kind and gentle with others because you see them as God sees them. Kindness and gentleness are two qualities that are sorely lacking in modern society. I often sense that some believe it is a sign of weakness to be kind and gentle with others. I have even heard people say they believe displaying kindness to others, unless they have specifically done something good to them first, is a sign of weakness, vulnerability, or softness. Those folks believe that showing others you are weak, vulnerable or soft can in turn make you a target for attack. In actuality, exemplifying the fruit of the Spirit is a strength, not a weakness. Walking in peace through every circumstance will allow you to be an example of God's joy in your life. It is God's joy that gives us strength in every situation.

In order to live and operate in the real world, we must actually love. Loving others is not optional. It is a requirement--a commandment. God as sovereign Lord has a right to be obeyed. Love is even one of the Ten Commandments. The scripture in Deuteronomy 10: 12-13 states, "And now, Israel, what doth the Lord thy God require of thee, but to fear the Lord thy God, to walk in all His ways and to love Him, and to serve the Lord thy God with all thy heart and with all thy soul, to keep the commandments of the Lord, and His statutes which I command thee this day for thy good." The commandment is to love the Lord your God with all your heart and all your soul and all your mind, which will help you to love your neighbor as you love yourself. When God gave the Ten Commandments to Moses, He knew that if we loved God with all our hearts and if we loved our neighbors like we love ourselves, the rest of the commandments would be a piece of cake to follow.

God is very serious about us loving one another. No matter the situation—no matter what people are saying, what they're doing, what they're *not* doing, how they are are acting, we must love. After dealing with some very difficult and negative people, I began to feel that loving others *no matter what* was just not possible in the world in which we live now. People in Biblical days surely must have had an easier time of this than we do now, right? Today's world is so complicated. Sin appears to be running rampant, day and night. As I listen to the evening news reports I often leave the room in disgust and horror. Just when I think I have heard the nastiest thing one human being could do to another, I hear another story that is even worse. How can we love people who are doing such horrible and unimaginable things? Can we really do this in a practical way that is not phony or hypocritical?

The prophet Jeremiah grappled with the same question. Jeremiah 15:15-21 begins with Jeremiah praising God. Jeremiah then reminds God of all the things he has done for God's sake and about all the sacrifices he has made for God. Then Jeremiah moves into complaining about how terrible the people around him are treating him. In his anguish,

Jeremiah accuses God of having a love that is like a seasonal brook; running full at some times and then going bone dry at others.

In other words, Jeremiah accused God of being unreliable, undependable, and unpredictable.

Jeremiah was unhappy because of the people's lack of response to his message, and because of their persecution of him personally. But look at God's beautiful response to Jeremiah, beginning in verse 19: He told Jeremiah to "separate what is precious from what is worthless."

To separate the good from the bad.

To separate what is pure from what is vile.

In other words, you have to separate what is real from what is fantasy or unreal. You have to separate the truth from lies. Do not just push your feelings *aside*; push them *out* if they do not line up with God's

Word, which commands us to love. God had called Jeremiah to influence the people around him. Instead, Jeremiah was letting the people influence him in a negative way. God told Jeremiah, "If you come back to me I will strengthen and empower you and enable you to be stronger in a way you never envisioned." The good news is, that word from the Lord was not just for Jeremiah years ago; it is for you and me today.

You already know this, but the love business is not always easy. The challenge to love everyone is not an easy one. It is easy to love those who love us. It is easy to love those who agree with us. I am not referring here to liking others; I am talking about loving them. This requirement to love becomes particularly difficult when we are required to love the mean, ugly, nasty, impossible, unlovable people in our lives. The ones who do not agree with us. The ones who despise us, often for no good reason. The ones who judge us or falsely accuse us.

But it turns out these are the ones God especially calls us to love.

I really struggled with this requirement to love all others. And, I'd bet if you were honest you would admit that you, too, have struggled with this requirement at some point during your life. If you are like I was, you have an offense scale. My scale ran from #1 to #10. An offense that registered between #1 and #5 was not too bad. I could get over these things pretty easily. I was usually able to shake this level of offense off pretty quickly and move on without much, if any, bitterness. But oh my goodness, if the offense registered #6 to #9 on my scale, you were moving onto shaky ground with me! There have even been a few people in my life who have committed a #10 scale offense against me. I was so angry with those number #10 offenders that I said if I ever saw them again I could not be responsible for what I might do. I rationalized that I would exact my own vengeance and then ask God to forgive me afterward. I hope it does not impact your theology here if I am transparent and honest. Remember, we hide from others, but never from God. He knows and sees all. I had a scale, but God has no such scale. When He commanded us to love one another, He wasn't talking about loving those who commit only minor offenses against us. And how do we know this? We know it because *His* love covers EVERY OFFENSE. The Scripture states in 1Peter 4:8, "And above all things, have fervent charity among yourselves; for charity shall cover the multitude of sins."

I really wanted to follow Gods command. I really wanted to love like God wanted me to—to love like He does. I just could not do it on my own. I began to cry out to the Lord, "How can I do this on a daily basis? How can I do this with a sincere heart?" The Lord gave me an answer. He instructed me to break up the word LOVE and look at it in a different way.

In order to really love people where they are, in whatever state we find them we have to

L – Let
O – Others'
V – Value
E – Exceed.

Let the value you place on other people exceed everything, anything, all things, at all times. Let the value you place on others exceed their offenses against you. Let the value you place on them exceed your disappointments. Let the value you place on others exceed your rejection of them—and their rejection of you. Let the value you place on others exceed your own hurt feelings. Let the value you place on others exceed your judgment of them. Let the value you place on them exceed your fear, or your desire for vengeance. Let the value you place on them exceed your anger, your bitterness, or the fact that they were unjustified in what they did. Let the value you place on others exceed the knowledge that you did not deserve what happened to you. Let the value you place on others exceed your own pain, your anguish, your agony. Learn to see your offenders the way God sees them—the way God sees us.

And how does God see us?

God lets His love exceed our sins. God lets His purpose exceed our failures. God lets His forgiveness exceed our sins. God lets His mercy and grace exceed our disobedience and rebellion.

Real love requires doing the "hard" things in life. It requires us to push past our own pain, our own disappointments, our own frustrations, to do what God commands. And God commands us to love and forgive others. Despite the level of offense against us--despite our reactions and our feelings, we must obey God. How can we say that we love God if we will not do what He says to do? Jesus Himself stated in John 13:34-35, "A new commandment I give unto you, that ye love one another; as I have loved you, that ye also love one another. By this shall all men know that ye are my disciples, if ye have love one to another."

1 John 5:2-3 says, "By this we know that we love the children of God, when we love God, and keep His commandments. For this is the love of God, that we keep His commandments: and His commandments are not grievous."

The Scripture in John 15:1-17 shows Jesus teaching His disciples about our connection to God and how this applies to love. Jesus says, "I am the true vine, and My Father is the vinedresser" (In other words, the one responsible for taking care of the vines.)

"Every branch in Me that does not bear any fruit He takes away; and every branch that bears fruit He prunes it so that it may bear even the more fruit. You are already clean because of the word, which I have spoken to you. Abide in Me and I in you." (In other words, "Stay totally connected to me and I will stay totally connected to you.")

"As the branch cannot bear fruit of itself unless it abides in the vine, so neither can you unless you abide in Me. I am the vine, you are the branches; he who abides in Me and I in him bears much fruit, for apart from Me you can do nothing. If anyone does not abide in Me, he is thrown away as a branch and dries up; and they gather them, and cast them into the fire and they are burned." (In other words, "Apart from Me, your value is greatly diminished.")

"If you abide in Me, and My words abide in you, ask whatever you wish, and it will be done for you. My Father is glorified by this, that you bear much fruit, and so prove to be My disciples. Just as the Father has loved Me, I have also loved you; abide in my love. If you keep my commandments, you will abide in My love; just as I have kept My Father's commandments and abide in His love. These things I have spoken to you so that My joy may be in you, and that your joy may be made full."

And then Jesus says, "This is My commandment, that you love one another, just as I have loved you. Greater love has no one that this, that one lay down his life for his friends. You are my friends if you do what I command you. No longer will I call you slaves, for the slave does not know what his master is doing; but I have called you friends for all things that I have heard from My Father I have made known to you. You did not choose Me but I chose you and appointed you that you would go and bear fruit and that your fruit would remain, so that whatever you ask of the Father in My name He may give to you."

Jesus sums it up with, "This I command you, that you love one another."

We have the choice to follow God or not. He will not zap us with lightening from Heaven if we decide not to love others. Instead, we experience something even more serious by choosing not to obey His command to love: we injure our own communion with our Heavenly Father. By failing to obey this command, we miss out on the joy of living the way He wants us to live. We miss the peace in our own hearts. We miss the abundant blessings He has for us.

We even risk having our prayers go unanswered.

The Scriptures say if you come to the altar and you have offense against your brother (or sister), you must leave the altar and go settle that issue first, then come back to the altar to ask what you will of God. Matthew 5:23-24 says, "Therefore if thou bring thy gift to the altar, and go thy way; first be reconciled to thy brother and then come and offer thy gift."

The requirement to love is not negotiable. It is not open to interpretation. It is not open to compromise. It is not seasonal. Ask God to help you learn how to operate in the love world. Remember the Word of God is more *real* than your feelings are about anything.

This is how we learn to live and operate in the real world.

STUDY AND DISCUSSION QUESTIONS – CHAPTER TWO

1. Reflect on a situation in which it felt impossible for you to love another person.

2. What about that situation made it so difficult?

3. Did you end up loving that person out of obedience to God?

4. What helped you to "get over it" and move on?

5. Do you love that person now? Why or why not?

6. What could you have done differently to move toward love?

7. What did you find helpful in moving toward loving them?

8. Think of a family member, co-worker, neighbor, or friend, whom you currently know is struggling with this love issue. Write their name on a piece of paper.

9. What can you share from this chapter to help that person?

10. Take a few minutes to say a prayer and ask God to help you and the name on your paper to learn to love more. Ask Him to increase your ability to love. Ask Him to help you understand the importance of love. Ask Him to deepen your reservoir of love so that you can enjoy the blessing that comes with obeying Him.

CHAPTER THREE

OPERATING IN THE WORLD OF WAR

We are very familiar with war.

Webster's Ninth New Collegiate Dictionary defines *war* as strife, conflict, and antagonism. It's a struggle between opposing forces, for a particular end. It is enmity. It is intentional. It is targeted. It is deliberate. It is meant to inflict harm. It is meant to create upset or discomfort. It is meant to disrupt. It is meant to destroy.

Unfortunately, there is war all around us. Sometimes we can even create war in our own bodies (through unhealthy eating and lifestyles), in our own minds (through fear and hatred) and even in our souls (through unforgiveness and bitterness). I think it is safe to say that there is war in the economy, war on the job, war among the nations, and war in our homes. There is war among families; there is war in the church. War, war, WAR! As much as we would like to escape it, the unfortunate truth is that war is always there. If you are looking for a battle, you do not have to look far. For most people, war is all around them.

Let's look at each of these.

There is war in the economy. In the United States of America (my home), our war is with the demonic strongman of greed. Greed is constantly rearing his ugly head and trying to influence all the components of our society. American businesses are greedy for profits so they do things that are not right, not ethical, not honest. They send work overseas where they can pay citizens of third world countries less than half of what they would have to pay American workers. And although this work *might* benefit those third world citizens, it often results in inhumane conditions such as unreasonably long hours, child labor, harsh and unsafe working environments, and lower than standard wages, just to name a few. Many companies looking for ways to cut corners or maximize their profits decide to use inferior materials and allow poor workmanship. This philosophy has resulted in products being placed on the market, which have caused injury and even death to some purchasers and users of said products. Greed wars against the conscience. Greed wars against a sense of compassion and empathy. Greed wars against justice. Greed wars against integrity. Unfortunately this strongman is pervasive in many Americans, but its power is not confined to the United States. Greed is a universal epidemic.

There is war on the job. Lord knows, I have seen my share of this. I seem to have had the fortune--or shall I say, misfortune—of working with some of the nastiest, most mean- spirited people alive. These people were arrogant, racist, self-absorbed, merciless, and seemingly void of justice and compassion. I have worked for supervisors who lie, manipu- late, self-exalt and self-protect at all costs. There were many days that I cried out to God and asked Him where His justice and vengeance were.

I know many people in all types of occupations. I know physicians, lawyers, speech therapists, physical therapists, pharmacists, advertising representatives, marketing personnel, insurance agents, salesmen and women, factory workers, television producers, writers, teachers, police officers, information technology workers, Foreign Service personnel, artists, entrepreneurs, and government workers on the Federal, State, and local levels. There is one thread that seems to run through each of their experiences on the job:

Most of them do not love their jobs.

Digging a little deeper, though, the truth is that mainly, they do not like the people at their jobs. They usually like and understand the work itself. They are usually skilled, trained, and educated to do what they do, and their work may even be rewarding and fulfilling for them personally. The problems, however, often seem to stem back to some person or maybe several people on the jobsite. This could be a supervisor or it could be a colleague, peer, subordinate, or client.

I remember that in some of my own challenging situations, I had to summon up all the "Spirit of Jesus Christ" within me just to keep from doing or saying what I really, really wanted to do or say. Some of these people were so deserving of a piece of my mind! But thanks be to God, who always causes us to triumph! Because of the Holy Spirit and His ever-present help, I was reminded that if my mind was not the *mind of Christ* in a particular situation, then I did not need to give it to anybody. I needed to keep my thoughts and feelings to myself. I needed to allow God to work on me. I needed to allow God to work on them. I needed to allow God to war in this situation, because ultimately the battle was His anyway and He sure knows how to win a war.

There is war in the nations. Nations with land want more land. Nations with oil want to protect it. Nations without bombs want them. Nations with bombs want to keep those who don't have bombs from getting bombs. Nations with various ethnic groups are grappling with how to share and coexist peacefully. Nations without enough resources are cannibalizing each other. Nations with power often exploit those without power. Nations with dictatorships are warring to keep it that way rather than relinquish power. Nations with democracies are struggling to maintain it. Nations with diminishing resources are strategizing how to get more, often at the expense of some other nation or the poorest among their own. Nations are at war around religious beliefs, financial issues, philosophical differences, political opinions, and concerns over natural resources. Nations are at war.

There is war in the home and in the family. Husbands and wives are against each other, to the point of abuse, unfaithfulness, and broken families. Mothers are against their children. Fathers are against their children. Aunts and uncles, nephews, nieces, and cousins, brothers and sisters, war against each other. News reports are full of stories about mothers drowning, shooting, stabbing, starving, beating, neglecting, and mistreating their children. News reports are full of stories about Fathers who mistreat and abandon Mothers and the terrible impact this has on the children. News reports are full of accounts of extended family members who molest, cheat, and harm other family members. News reports are full of stories about infidelity, adultery, divorce, abuse and abandonment. There are stories of human trafficking, incest, prostitution, rape, too often in connection with some sort of family component, in which someone who was supposed to be trusted the most inflicted the most injury. This is particularly harmful and devastating because the home is the place where there should be acceptance and love for all who dwell within. There should be love and peace in the home. There should be unity in the home. This is the place where God's love should be taught and modeled. The home is where love should be demonstrated at all costs. When there is war in the home the pain can be unbearable.

There is even war in the church. There is strife among the congregation, strife between deacons and trustees. There is strife with and against the pastor, and strife between the pastor and the officers. There is strife between those in leadership. There is competition on the ministerial staff. There is conflict about the church budget. There are complaints about what the pastor is preaching, and about what the pastor is not preaching. There are denominational divisions. Doctrinal divisions. Racial divisions. Ethnic divisions. There are class or status divisions. There are economic divisions. The church is divided over many issues.

We are called to be a people of war, but we are to war in the right way. We are to war in the Spirit for those around us who are yet unsaved. We are to war against sin and depravity. We are to war against any force frustrating or blocking our ability to come into a full and mature understanding of God. 1 Timothy 6:12 calls us to "fight the good fight of faith; lay hold of the eternal life whereunto thou art also called, and hast professed a good confession before many witnesses." Even the angels war on our behalf. When we pray, our answer is often dispatched immediately by God; however, the angels often have to war against demonic opposition to bring it to full manifestation. The Scriptures state in Daniel 10:12-13, "Then he said unto me, Fear not Daniel, for from the first day that thou didst set thine heart to understanding and to chasten thyself before thy God, your words were heard, and I am come for thy words. But the prince of the kingdom of

Persia withstood me for one and twenty days; but lo Michael, one of the chief princes came to help me, and I remained there with the kings of Persia." The Lord wants us to understand that this occurrence was not only true in the days of Daniel.

Although we must . . . we shall . . . we *will* war, we must be careful to do so in the manner that God would have us war. In other words, we are not to war against each other or with each other; we are to war on behalf of the purposes and goals of God. We are to war for peace. We are to war for justice. We are to war for equality. We are to war for salvation. We are to war for compassion and mercy. We are to war for the preaching and teaching of the Holy Gospel. We are to war for God's provision and prosperity for His people. We are to war for God's protection, His passion, and His purposes.

It is only by learning how to war according to the purposes and plans of God that we will be able to live and operate in the real world.

STUDY AND DISCUSSION QUESTIONS – CHAPTER THREE

1. Reflect upon a time when you felt you were in a situation of war.

2. Describe this situation.

3. Have you obtained the victory?

4. If so, what did you do to help you obtain the victory?

5. If not, what can you do to move toward victory?

6. Describe what has happened to you mentally, physically, and spiritually as you have gone through this conflict.

7. If given a chance to do anything different, what would it be?

8. What role has someone else played in your victory?

9. What lessons did you learn through this conflict?

10. Thank God for this opportunity to know Him better through this war situation in your life. Give Him glory for your victory, or, give Him glory for the victory that you are certain will come. Thank Him for His faithfulness through it all.

CHAPTER FOUR

ALL WEEK LONG

It is very easy to be a good Christian on Sunday morning, Sunday afternoon, and even on Sunday night. It does not take much energy, effort, or stamina. More strength is required to remain faithful to our Christian teachings and lifestyle Monday through Saturday. Opportunities abound for us to get off course, off focus, off message. There are innumerable challenges, obstacles, traps, and tricks that come our way and attempt to keep us from remaining consistent, reliable Christians. In fact, this is often the very thing that makes it difficult to win souls for Christ, especially among our friends and family. They are the ones closest to us, and therefore have the opportunity to witness firsthand our instability, and often our hypocrisy.

It is difficult to remain consistent as we walk out our faith on a daily basis. The good news is that we do not have to remain consistent under our own strength. The Scripture in Philippians 1:6 states, "Being confident of this very thing, that He which hath begun a good work in you will perform it until the day of Jesus Christ." It is God who, first of all, established what our unique and particular "good work" would be.

It is also God who begins the good work in us, not we ourselves. The Scripture in Jeremiah 1:5 states, "Before I formed thee in the belly I knew thee. And before thou camest forth out of the belly I sanctified thee; and I ordained thee a prophet to the nations." God not only established what a good work would be for each and every one of us, He also informed us that He is the one who will perfect it. In other words, He would support it, protect it, nurture it, encourage it, and establish it. God is the one who will do within us whatever it takes to allow His word to come to pass in our lives.

It is His good pleasure to assure that His purposes for our lives are fulfilled. God does this in a multitude of ways: He plants some of us in families where the Gospel is lived out and we are allowed to grow up with fear of and reverence for the Lord. For others, He allows our paths to cross with peers and colleagues who will assist us in remaining steady in the things of God. For some, He allows the occupation we choose and pursue to be our compass for walking in the right paths of God. And of course there is the church, which provides a foundation and an anchoring for being committed and abounding in the work of the Lord. The scripture states in 1 Corinthians 15:58, "Therefore, my beloved brethren, be ye steadfast, immoveable, always abounding in the work of the Lord, for as much as ye know that your labour is not in vain in the Lord."

I really learned some of the things the Lord uses to help us make it through the week when I had the honor of participating in a foreign mission trip to South Africa. While there, we ministered in churches, schools, communities, hospitals, and jails. It was one of the most impactful experiences of my life. The levels of suffering and of hunger for Jesus were beyond what I had ever seen or experienced in the United States. It was during one of the many church services in which we participated that I heard a South African pastor identify one way we can remain faithful during our daily walk. This pastor told us that we should be taking notes every time we come to church or any place where we are likely to hear the word of God. Why is this, you might ask? The reason is because as Christians we believe that when we come to church we are coming there to hear from God. The singing, the display of art (dance, drama, etc.) and the preaching of the Word are all vehicles by which God ministers to us. He speaks through all of these vehicles. Therefore, we should be taking notes so we can capture His precious words and messages to us. Think of this analogy: When we go to school, we attend classes so we can learn and grow. The teacher has been trained, selected and placed there to assist us with our learning, our training and our growth. As the teacher speaks, we take notes so we do not miss any important points. After taking the notes, we should become more familiar with the subject area and therefore be able to pass the test. If we do not take good notes and reflect upon the lectures and the lessons, we may not be able to pass the quizzes and tests when they come.

Life is full of tests that we must pass. God gives us instruction through His ministry to us--His preached word, His music, His dance ministry, His drama ministry--to teach us how to pass the tests in life and how to remain steadfast and consistent. When we fail to take notes in church we are in essence saying that what is being provided is not valuable enough for us to remember and reflect upon. So, if we believe our Pastor is anointed and sent by God, then we also have to believe that our Pastor is hearing from God while preparing and delivering the preached message. We should believe that the word the minister delivers is the result of having spent time preparing in prayer and in the presence of God. If we believe this to be true--that each sermon is the result of hearing from God-- then what is provided is from God and therefore valuable to each and every one of us. If it is valuable and from God, why wouldn't we want to be able to reflect upon the words of God throughout the days, weeks, months, and years to come? I encourage you, as that South African pastor encouraged us, not to continue coming to church or other ministry events without a pen and paper or some mechanism by which to take notes. I guarantee that something you will hear or see will become exactly what you need when your life tests come along.

This will help you to learn how to live and operate in the real world . . . not just on Sundays, but throughout each and every day of your life.

STUDY AND DISCUSSIONS QUESTIONS - CHAPTER FOUR

1. Reflect upon a time when you found it difficult to remain steadfast or consistent.

2. What person or situation tested you in this way?

3. How did you respond to this test?

4. Were you victorious?

5. Explain what you do now to remain victorious.

6. If you were not victorious, explain why.

7. What can you do differently to remain faithful?

8. What do you believe are common obstacles for most believers in their quest to remain faithful and consistent?

9. If you could turn back time or give advice to new believers, what advice would you give to help them remain consistent or steadfast?

10. Take a minute to thank God for His wisdom, assistance, and support as we all strive to walk out this Christian life in a way that would please Him and give Him glory.

Chapter Five

WITH OUR CONFESSIONS

*D*ay in and day out, we communicate. Often that involves talk. Some talk with their mouths. Others talk with their hands, as in the case of sign language. We are constantly conversing with someone about something. Your occupation, your location, your status, your gender—these all determine to whom you talk, what you talk about, and how much you talk. The average American speaks thousands of words per day (Swaminathan, 2007). A study led by Dr. Matthias Mehl, an Associate Professor in the Department of Psychology at the University of Arizona's College of Social and Behavioral Sciences, shows that on average, women speak 16,215 words per day and men speak 15,669 per day (Mehl, 2007). The study also found one person who spoke as little at 795 words per day, and

63

another who spoke 47,000 words in a day. This information, of course, is not true for every person, every day. I am sure these quantities are further correlated with a number of factors, such as occupation, culture, background, upbringing, family dynamics, and health (i.e. a health condition impacting the ability to speak), just to name a few.

Words and language (including sign language) are the tools used by a sender to convey information or concepts to a receiver. Linguistics is the scientific study of language and its form, meaning, and context, including phonetics, phonology, morphology, syntax, semantics, pragmatics, and historical linguistics. It is the study of the structure and development of language in general, as well as the study of how language works. People who are hearing impaired or sight impaired also use language through the use of sign language or tactile sign language--braille. Language is connected to communication. Communication takes place in every culture.

There are some occupations that require you to talk quite a bit on a regular basis, i.e. teachers, salespersons, and ministers. You may even be in a position where you have others who talk for you or on your behalf. There are cultural issues that impact how many, by whom, and which words are spoken. Even in 2017 there are many places around the world where cultural mores impact communication..

We talk to others, we talk to ourselves, and most importantly, we talk to God. The words we speak to others can bring instruction, healing, sorrow, joy, wounds, encouragement or defeat.

The words we speak bring hope or despair. Victory or defeat.

Our words can solve problems or exacerbate them. Our words can bind, or break.

Words soothe or scathe; they restore or destroy. Words can be weapons or tools, which alleviate or inflict pain. Words invoke both laughter and tears. They have the power to fill or empty the heart. Words build up or tear down. They can divide and separate and they can meld people together. Words bring peace and sometimes war. Words feed understanding, but can also create confusion. Words may build opportunities for trust or foster distrust and suspicion. Words inflame or words calm. Words can encourage action or create inaction.

Words bring life.

Words bring death.

The power of words in immeasurable.

The Bible says much about the power of words. We read in James 3:1-12:

> Let not many of you become teachers, my brethren, knowing that as such we will incur a stricter judgment because of the words you speak to others. For we all stumble in many ways. If anyone does not stumble in what

he says he is a perfect man, able to bridle the whole body as well. In other words, your mouth can take control of your entire body. Now if we put the bits into the horses' mouths so that they will obey us, we can direct the horse's entire body as well. Look at the ships at sea also, though they are so great and can be driven by strong winds, are still directed by a very small rudder whatever the inclination of the pilot desires. So also my friends the tongue is a small part of the body, and yet it can boast of great things. See how even a great and mighty forest is set aflame by such a small fire. And the tongue is a fire, the very world of iniquity; the tongue is the one thing that is set among our members that has the power to defile the entire body, and set on fire the course of our life. The tongue can be set on fire by hell itself. For every species of beasts and birds of reptiles and creatures of the sea, is tamed and has been tamed by the human race. But no one can tame the tongue. It is a restless evil and full of deadly poison.

With it we can bless our Lord and Father and with it we can curse men, who have been made in the likeness of God. It is possible from the same mouth for both blessing and cursing to come out. My brothers and sisters these things ought not to be this way. Does a fountain send out from the same opening both fresh and bitter water? Can a fig tree, my brothers and sisters produce olives or a vine produce figs? Nor can salt water produce fresh.

So often, we speak thoughtless words and phrases without considering their impact or their power. But the Bible is clear that the power of life and death is in the power of the tongue. I started teaching my children from an early age that there was power in their words. I encouraged them to speak life and victory into their situations, rather than defeat and loss. I taught them that words are not powerless. Words are not frivolous. Words are not devoid of ability. God Himself spoke the world and all of creation into existence. Genesis Chapter 1 is filled with evidence that God spoke and all of creation came into existence.

By the very word of God, things happened. What was not in existence suddenly *became something* at the words of God. What was devoid and dark took shape and became light at the words of God. It was Jesus who spoke to the disciples and followers about the coming of the Messiah and what that would mean for their lives. It was angels who spoke to Mary and to Daniel. It was the serpent who spoke to Eve and convinced her to sin against God.

Never underestimate the power of your words. The Lord wants us to see the value in words—to use them in accordance with the power they hold. He wants us to use our words wisely—to uplift rather than tear down.

To bring truth rather than lies; to bring unity rather than division.

To speak His holy Word--not what the world or the culture says.

The Lord wants us to speak as if the Word of God is real truth and all else is merely perception or feelings. Perception and feelings are subject to change, but the Word of the Lord will not change. The Holy Word of God will always have power. It will always change circumstances. It will always produce results. It will always do what God has ordained. This is why the Holy Word of God is the language we must speak. These are the words we must place in our mouths and send out into our lives each day. These are the words we must give to others. These are the words that will bring us life and not death. These are the words that will provide hope out of hopelessness.

These are the words that will bring us to a place where we are able to operate in the real world.

STUDY AND DISCUSSION QUESTIONS – CHAPTER FIVE

1. Reflect upon the words you have spoken in the last 24 hours. Did the majority of your words create life or death- in you or others?

2. What do you remember about the words spoken in your home as a child?

3. Describe one situation in which you could have or should have used words differently.

4. What one thing have you heard or said has impacted your life so much that you never forgot it?

5. Why did those words impact you in this way?

6. What words best describe your current situation in your home, job, school, community, etc.?

7. What words would you want to describe your current situation in your home, job, school, community, etc. ?

8. What one word has meant the most to you during your life?

9. Thank God for His wisdom and insight about the power of words. Now think of 7 words that you will commit to speak to yourself for one week. Choose words that will bring life, healing, hope, peace, and favor into your life. Commit to speak one of these words a day for the next 7 days, and watch how the power of God impacts you.

You can write these words on a piece of paper or an index card and put them around the house if you like – just do not forget to pro-claim them to yourself each day for the next seven days. (Be sure to share the results with your group at the next meeting.)

CHAPTER SIX

FIXING YOUR FOCUS

We were created to bring God glory and fulfill the work He has called us to do. There is a purpose for everyone-- every human being on the earth. It doesn't matter whether you knew your father or not. It doesn't matter whether you are "legitimate" or not. It doesn't matter whether you are a child of divorce. No matter the situation of your birth, you were born to bring God glory. In order to do this, you must fulfill your destiny.

The way to fulfill your destiny, first, is to ask God what your purpose is. He made you and He knows better than anyone else what your purpose entails.

When I asked God how to fulfill my own destiny, He gave me an acrostic to assist me in my quest. He showed me:

D Discover and Develop

E Every

S Skill

T That God Has Placed

I

    IN

N

Y You

To sum that up, the Lord instructed me to take some time out--first to discover, and then to develop--every skill and talent that He had already placed within me. I had to find that thing that I loved. I did; it was teaching. In fact, I loved teaching so much that I would do it even if no one paid me to do it. I have a natural aptitude and gift for teaching. Because I do it well, I realized that was part of the reason I loved it so much. I believe the Lord Himself put that love and desire within me because it was part of His ultimate plan for my life.

So once I discovered this, what did I do?

I began to teach.

I would teach anywhere an opportunity presented itself. I would even teach in church to the empty pews, believing that one day, the Lord would put me in front of people hungry for His Word.

What is it that you love to do? What are you good at? What would you do, even if no one paid you to do it?

Your lifestyle should reflect your destiny, your direction. It should reflect your purpose. Your passion. Your position on the things of God.

The way we live reflects two different components. There are some things we have control over, and some things over which we do not have control. We cannot control our place of birth or death, but we can control--to some degree--where we live between the points of birth and death. We get to make some choices about these things. Now I say *some* choices because I realize that due to financial situations, health situations, and political situations, some of our choices may be limited. Even though these things are true, I know that with God all things are possible, and God is able to help us overcome the limiting circumstances in our lives.

When I think of destiny, I think of the tasks we were put on this earth to fulfill--the assignments we were given in heaven before being placed in the wombs of our mothers.

Our reasons for occupying this place and time on the earth.

The acrostic the Lord gave me to help me understand how to fulfill my destiny was to understand that I had to:

Develop

Every

Skill and

Talent

IN

You.

In Jeremiah chapter 1, we see that The Lord knew us while we were yet in our mothers' wombs.

We see that we are fearfully and wonderfully made.

We are made in the image of God. Is not the image of something a reflection of the original? God has a plan to give each of us a hope and a future. This hope and this future will allow us to fulfill our destinies.

We see in the scriptures that God is creative, wonderful, smart, talented, gifted . . . so why wouldn't He put those qualities in His prized creation – us? Each and every human being on the earth from the beginning of time has been given some skills and some talents, without exception. Matthew 25:15 reasons that God gives talents to all. Some receive five talents, some two talents, some one talent. This should give us the confidence that regardless of our station in life, we have not been left out. We have not been born without a destiny. We all have received some sort of skill and talent that we are called to develop. Sometimes we know our gifts from an early age and are able to develop and fine tune them as we grow through our childhood and mature into adulthood. This allows us to become a mighty vessel for God to use in building His kingdom here on earth. It is wonderful when parents recognize the God-given skills and talents in their children and help their children grow and develop in those areas. This is the real job of a parent--to prepare the next generation to fulfill their destiny in the Lord. There are other times when people do not discover their God-given skills and talents until their adult years. The Lord is able to assist us at any age to develop our skills and talents, and He is able to send people, resources, and support to help us as needed. It is never too late. What is a real tragedy in life is when a person never finds out what their God given skills and talents are and never develops them or utilizes them for the benefit of the kingdom of God. Sadder still, there are those who do recognize their God-given skills and talents and use them for the works of Satan, darkness, and evil. Many in the entertainment industry have used their gifts to influence people toward darkness instead of the marvelous knowledge of Jesus Christ.

Developing every skill and talent God has placed in you is not always easy. The work of development requires studying. 2 Timothy 2:15 tells us that we should be workmen who study to show ourselves approved. We should be workmen who are not ashamed because we are able to rightly divide the Word of God--the Word of truth. Developing our skills and talents can also require us to pray and fast along with our studying and preparation. Developing our skills and talents so we can fulfill our destiny involves self-sacrifice. These are the ingredients that help make us strong Christians. These are the things that will allow us to fix our focus in order to fulfill our destiny in the Lord.

It is important to note that developing your skills and talents is not a one-time action. There is no end point. There is no point in time when you can mark it on a calendar or sit down and say, "Whew, I am now totally finished developing every skill and talent that God has placed inside me; now I have fulfilled my destiny." Mature Christians know from reading Hebrews 13:8 that although the Lord is the same yesterday, today, and forevermore, His will for our lives does evolve--and He allows it to evolve, often in connection with our own free will.

For example, let's just say you have a great singing voice. After graduating from high school, you must choose between two roads: You may join a local band, sing at gigs, and possibly make a career of music at some level. Or, you might go to a music conservatory, learn to compose, sing opera, and become a professional singer, touring with a world-renowned opera company. God can and will bless you on either of these pathways, but it is important to seek God for the pathway that represents His will for your life. Neither pathway is right or wrong in and of itself, but God has a pathway that He desires for each of us that will help us to fulfill our destiny in Him and help us contribute to building the kingdom of God here on earth--which will prepare for the return of our Lord and Savior Jesus Christ.

Find your fulfillment in living out God's purposes for your life, using the gifts He has given you. It is only by doing this that we can truly live and operate in the real world.

STUDY AND DISCUSSION QUESTIONS – CHAPTER SIX

1. Commit to take some time today to seek the Lord about what your destiny is. Ask Him to show you what skills and talents He has placed within you and how He wants you to use them.

2. How will you know that you have fulfilled your destiny?

3. Name some important people God has placed in your path to help you fulfill your destiny.

4. Are you called to assist someone else with his or her destiny?

5. If so, in what way?

6. Have you ever known someone who doesn't know their skills and talents?

7. Have you ever known someone who doesn't know their destiny?

8. Have you ever seen someone squander their skills or their destiny?

9. How did you respond?

10. What one thing, if any, would you change about how you are fulfilling your own destiny?

CHAPTER SEVEN

EVERY GOOD QUESTION DESERVES AN ANSWER

Who on earth has not been questioned?

The questions begin the day we are born. We are questioned as part of our daily existence. Our parents and guardians question us as part of raising us. Our teachers question us as part of teaching us. Our community questions us regarding our participation in the larger unit. Our churches question us as part of our participation in the body of Christ. Our friends question us as part of our relationships. Our spouses and significant others question us as part of their ongoing relationships with us. Our governmental officials question us about our adherence to various rules, regulations, and laws. Our supervisors, managers, and employers question us as part of our employment. We often even question ourselves to make sure we are doing and thinking the right things. But I want to make us aware that not only do we face questions from our earthly relationships; the Lord questions us also. You may wonder, "How can that be true? What kinds of questions can the Lord ask me?"

How does the Lord ask us? He asks us through His holy Word and through His ongoing relationship with us:

"Wilt thou be made whole?"

"Is life only food and drink?"

Is man like a puppet with no ability to change the direction of God? Who are we anyway? What was I put on earth to do?

We are questioned as part of our daily existence. The Lord questions us about our motives--our intentions--the condition of our hearts. In

Matthew 12:34, the scriptures tell us that out of the abundance of the heart the mouth speaks. We are questioned about our consciences. Are we living in a way that makes us feel good about our actions? Are we treating others the way we would like to be treated? Are we acting the way a Christian should? Are we responding to life's challenges in a way that shows we have faith in God? Do we repay evil for evil? Do we believe that God is able to help us conquer any enemy? Do we believe there is hope for every situation we face?

Let me explain fully what I mean when I say that God questions us. What I am stating is that I believe God challenges us through life's situations, circumstances, relationships, and events. He uses these points in our lives to bring us face-to-face with our belief systems. When we face various situations, we are forced to evaluate, question, and determine what we believe, what we feel, what we think, and what we will do from that point forward. We also often establish where we think God fits into the situation. It is at these points that God challenges us to examine our faith. He questions us to establish what it is that we really believe . . . and who it is that we really believe in. Will we believe God's Word or will we believe our situation? Will we trust His decision or will we trust our own intellect and analysis? Will we let fear drive our actions, or will we look to the Lord? Will we lean to our own understanding or fully lean on the Lord's wisdom?

These are the questions God puts before us.

And every good question deserves an answer.

We all love to ask why. We are taught to ask *why* as a part of our schooling and our early training from our parents. In fact, there once was an ad campaign for a national magazine that used the slogan, "Inquiring minds want to know." Asking, "why?" tends to make us feel better. Even though we may not like the answers, we often feel a sense of closure when we ask why. Asking the *why* question helps us exercise our intelligence and logical abilities. When you find out *why* something happened, you can then piece it together with other facts and information to come full circle with your thinking, or string multiple thoughts together to come to a conclusion.

When trouble comes into your life, do you tend to ask God, "Why?"

Why is this happening to me? Why me? Why this? Why now?

Why haven't my prayers been answered?

Why has my health turned bad?

Why isn't my family happy like the ones I see on television?

Why am I not able to get advancement on the job?

Why are my finances never able to meet all I believe I need?

Why can't I seem to tap into the true meaning of life?

Why can't I seem to find a spouse?

Why don't I know my purpose in God?

God has already told us in His Word that we will face tribulation, depression, heartache, disappointment, and betrayal. The Bible is full of accounts in which these things have happened. However, the Bible also tells us not to lose heart. Do not think it strange—in fact, James 1:2 instructs us to *count it all joy* when we fall into diverse temptations.

Our job is to ask God *what;* not *why.* What season it is? Is it time to plant or time to harvest? What am I supposed to learn from this experience? What should my reaction be to this situation? What am I supposed to do? What can I do to make sure that God gets the glory out of this situation?

It is in the answer that we find the place of blessing, grace, favor, and hope. When we face struggle, difficulty, fear, strife, or challenges and we are questioned about what we believe, it is then that our answer should be that we believe the Word of the Lord. Our answer should be that we will live in the real world--the world in which the Spirit of God rules supreme and the Word of God has authority over every situation and every circumstance. Our answer should be as it is written in Psalm 20:7--that some trust in horses, some trust in chariots, but our trust is in the Name of the Lord. Philippians 4:8 further states that we should think about things that are true, things that are honest, things that are just, things that are pure, things that are lovely, things that are of good report. If there be any praise or virtue, we must think on these things.

We must be prepared to answer the Lord's questions.

We must do this so we can successfully live in the real world.

STUDY AND DISCUSSION QUESTIONS – CHAPTER SEVEN

1. Have you ever felt the challenge or question of God in your life?

2. Have you ever felt that you did not measure up?

3. When, and why did you not feel that you measured up?

4. Have you ever watched a friend or relative face the challenge of God?

5. Did you play a role in assisting someone during this phase in his or her life?

6. If you could go back and revisit the last time you felt challenged by God, what would you change?

7. Do you feel stronger since that last experience?

8. If so, why? If not, why not?

9. How is the challenge of God different for new believers versus mature Christians?

10. What advice would you give both?

CHAPTER EIGHT

CHOOSING A GOD PLAN OVER A GOOD PLAN

We are all full of good plans, but every good plan is not a God plan. Man has a way that seems good but the end thereof is really destruction We all want to think that we have a plan for our lives but what we don't realize is that a good plan is never better than a God plan. Our only real happiness, our only real success, our only real fulfillment is wrapped up in a God plan, not a good plan.

Chapters 1-7 of the book of Joshua give an account of two men: One man, Joshua, knew and understood the importance of following God's plan. Another man, Achan, thought he had a good plan but later found out that a good plan is not the same thing as a God plan.

The setting was the city of Jericho, in the land of Canaan. As you may recall from the book of Joshua, Chapter1, Joshua had become the successor to Moses. Moses had led God's people, the Israelites, out of bondage in Egypt. After wandering for 40 years in the wilderness, a new generation of people are now ready to cross over the Jordan river, from the east side, and enter Canaan, their promised land. Moses trained Joshua, who proved that he was a man who was full of courage and consistent faith, and therefore a capable leader. The first major city the Israelites had to conquer was Jericho. Jericho was a walled city built around an oasis in the midst of a hot and isolated valley about 840 feet below sea level. Joshua and the people set out in their plan to conquer Jericho. Joshua was told to rise early in the morning and set out from the Acacia Grove to the Jordan River, where he and the people were to lodge for 3 days. They were to look for the Ark of the Covenant of the Lord God, and then set out for their promised land. Joshua was instructed to send the priests over the Jordan River first, and the people would follow later, after sanctifying themselves. The Ark was a symbol of God's presence and power. The account continues with all the Israelites crossing the Jordan River in the spring, when the banks of the Jordan River were overflowing. Many scholars believe that God chose this time when the river was at its highest to demonstrate His power by parting the water so that the entire nation could cross on dry ground. God showed His great power, using the miracle of timing and location, to allow His people to cross the river on dry ground. Joshua then received instruction to take 12 men from each of the 12 tribes of Israel, and have them gather 12 stones from the Jordan River, with which they were to build a memorial. This may have seemed insignificant, but God did not want the people to enter the new land unprepared. He wanted their focus to be on Him. He wanted them to remember that He was the one guiding them. The scriptures show the many steps Joshua followed to prepare the people to occupy the Promised Land.

Jericho was a city built thousands of years before Joshua's birth. This city was fortified with walls up to 25 feet high and 20 feet thick. Military soldiers guarding the city would stand on the top of the wall so they could see any impending threats for miles. Jericho was probably considered the most important city in the Jordan valley at the time. A symbol of military strength, the Canaanites likely believed Jericho was indestructible. Israel was to attack this city first so that its destruction would strike fear into the heart of everyone in Canaan. The defeat of Jericho would show the Canaanites that Israel's God was superior to the Canaanite gods and that He was the only one that was invincible. Further, they were to defeat Jericho not by their own strength, but by obedience to their all-powerful God. God gave Joshua detailed instructions regarding how to defeat Jericho, and Joshua and the people obeyed: Joshua commanded the priests to lead with the Ark of the Covenant, followed by seven priests carrying trumpets made of rams' horns. These men walked around the city for seven days. On the seventh day, they marched around the city seven times, blew their horns, and the people shouted. These actions caused the walls to fall flat, and the city of Jericho fell. The Israelites had a guaranteed victory because they followed God's plan rather than following their own plans. I am sure it must have seemed strange to some of them to follow this plan instead of going into battle, however I believe that God made it clear that the battle would depend on Him, and not on Israel's weapons, might, or expertise. These strange maneuvers were a test of the Israelites' willingness to follow God completely rather than rely on what made sense to them in their own plans. After Joshua conquered Jericho, he then went on to attack Ai.

Achan, on the other hand, lived out a different story. In Joshua chapters 6 and 7, the Lord God told the Israelites what they were to keep and what they were to destroy of the plunder from the city. The Israelites were instructed to destroy almost everything and everybody in Jericho. This was God executing judgement against the wickedness of the Canaanites, which included idolatry and rebellion against God. This wickedness, if not destroyed, had the potential to contaminate the faith and righteous living of the Israelites. Objects symbolic of a life of rebellion had to be removed. There were some specific items identified as accursed, or off limits, for the Israelites to keep. These included things like clothing, cattle, and idols. Achan, a man in the Israelite camp, decided it would be a better plan to keep some of the accursed things plundered from Jericho for himself. Consequently, when Joshua and his men attempted to take over the city of Ai, they were defeated and chased away by the men of Ai, resulting in 36 Israelite casualties. This was a direct result of Achan's sin and his disobedience to God's plan and instruction.

Specifically, the results of Achan's disobedience were as follows:

1. Many Israelite men were killed.
2. Israel's army lost their confidence due to fear.
3. Joshua began to question God.
4. God threatened to withdraw His presence and protection for the Israelites.
5. Achan and his family had to be destroyed.

Conversely, when Israel followed God's orders and eliminated the sin from their community the results were:

1. Encouragement from God.
2. Experiencing God's presence in future battles.
3. God's guidance and commitments/promise for future victories.
4. God's permission to keep some things from battle for themselves.

There are many lessons for us to glean from these scriptures. As you can see from examining these two stories, God does not want us just to do things we think are *good* ideas; He wants us to do things that are *God* ideas.

He wants us to be obedient. He wants us to follow His direction, His leading, because that is the path of safety.

This is the path of blessing and fulfillment.

This is the path of victory and prosperity.

This is the path of God's provision and protection

This is the path of exhibiting our passion for God; the path of fulfilling His purposes.

This is the path of peace.

Finding the *God plan* will lead us to the path of success. Success is the one thing everyone in the world wants--success for body, mind, and soul. We all describe it in different ways, but it is something everyone in the world wants. Some define it through money; others define it through fame. Some define it through access to power; others measure it by being able to meet their daily needs for food, clothes, and shelter. Some define success by their relationships. Some define success with beauty and physical attributes. Some measure success by earthly achievements and accolades. But the only real success is found in doing the will of our Father in Heaven--fulfilling our God-given purposes. This is how we live in the real world--the world where the Spirit of God reigns supreme, not a world where the flesh of men reigns. We must live in a real world where *God's* plans lead and guide us, rather than our own plans.

Another area where we must be careful to follow God's plan rather than our own good plan is in the area of our finances. God says it is He who multiplies (2 Corinthians 9:10). He promises, "Give and I will multiply what you give" (Malachi 3:10; Luke 6:38). Sow into the work of the Kingdom . . . sow into the local church. Sow when you have money, and sow when you have no money. Sow not only your money, but your time and your talents also. The work of the Kingdom needs all of these.

Money alone will not do it. If that were the case, the governments of the world could just provide a check and all problems would be solved. But when people are hungry, they may need transportation to the bank to cash the check. They will need a way to obtain groceries. They will need a mechanism for transforming those groceries into wholesome and filling meals for their families.

Money without time and talent is not enough.

Time without money and talent is not enough.

Talent without time and money are not enough.

Money. Time. Talents. These three really must work together.

God has told us that He is able to take our offering and provide a return that is equal to 30%, 60%, or 90% (Matthew 13:8; Matthew 25:14-30). He was able to take one jar of oil and multiply it enough to pay off the widow's debt (2 Kings 4). He is able to take one loaf of bread and five fish to feed thousands with scraps left over (Matthew 14:13-21). And just to make sure we did not think this was a fluke or some sort of anomaly He did miracles like this on more than one occasion (see

Matthew 15:29-39). We must follow His instructions regarding giving and we must have faith in His promises and His power to multiply.

There are many lessons for us contained in these scriptural accounts. We must guard against distractions and personal desires so that they will not keep us from experiencing success. We face many decisions in life; one lesson we see is that God will give His guidance if we will but ask Him, listen for His answers, and be careful to implement His instructions carefully. When we do this, we position ourselves for blessing, victory, and success. We must recognize and avoid interferences that would lead us to follow what we perceive as *good plans*.

As we see from the Holy Bible, there is no good plan more powerful or successful than a God plan. It is only by seeking His wisdom and following His instruction that we will be able to live and operate in the real world.

STUDY AND DISCUSSION QUESTIONS – CHAPTER EIGHT

1. Have you ever had your own plan, despite feeling that God may have wanted you to do something else?

2. If so, what was it? Why did you not follow Gods plan?

3. How did things turn out?

4. Have you ever chosen the *God plan*, despite friends and relatives urging you to follow a *good plan*?

5. How did they react to your decision?

6. How did things turn out when you were obedient to God's plan?

7. How did you know the difference between a *God plan* and a *good plan*?

8. What would be your advice to others trying to choose a *God plan* over a *good plan*?

9. Stop and say a prayer for someone you know who is at a decision point in their life right now. Pray that they choose the God plan and not just a good plan.

10. What do you think God wants to teach us about giving?

11. What do you think God wants to teach us about money?

12. Do you believe we can ever have too much money?

13. How should we handle the resources we receive?

14. Who makes the financial decisions in your household?

15. Define rich. Define poor.

16. Is it ok to be rich? Is it ok to be poor?

17. What is the ultimate purpose of money?

18. Why does the Bible state in 1 Timothy 6:10 that the love of money is the root of all evil?

19. Pray that God would put resources in your hands for the purposes of building His Kingdom

CHAPTER NINE

SOME MISTAKES ARE MORE COSTLY THAN OTHERS

*S*cripture assures us we were formed to do the will of our Father in Heaven, the Lord God (Joshua 9:3-15, Numbers 33:55, and Exodus 34:12).

Even when we know we were formed to do God's will, we all go astray. We make mistakes, we listen to the voices of others rather than the Lord's voice, and we forget things we know to do that are good and right.

We all forget to do things. I have forgotten to put on my work shoes and have run out of the house on my way to work, only to find out that I'm wearing my house slippers. (I might even have been able to get away with this, except that it happened on a day I had an important meeting!) I ride the subway to work, and that day, I was about halfway there before I thought to myself, "Wow, my feet sure feel great today!" One look at my feet explained it all. Instead of wearing those pointed-toe dress pumps or those stilettos (which, by the way, always hurt the feet, no matter what women say), I was wearing shoes that felt comfortable on my feet and allowed me not to have to think about foot pain.

I have forgotten to put on deodorant. Oh, I may have taken a shower and used fancy scented shower gel, then put on the matching scented body lotion, then used the matching scented perfume or bath splash, but had on *no deodorant*. And once again, I did not realize it until I was where I needed to be. When this happened to me, I just sat very still or tried not to raise my arms for any reason. On one particularly hot day when I had forgotten to put on my deodorant, I just stopped en-route to my destination and bought some deodorant from a nearby drug store.

I have the most patient husband in the world. I say this for many reasons. One reason is that my husband is very careful with the financial records of the household. My husband likes to balance the checkbook to the very penny. And then there is me. I have, on occasion, forgotten to make deposits at the bank. I have walked around for days with a deposit in my purse. After a few days have passed, my husband will ask for the deposit slip so that he can reconcile the records . . . and *that* is when I remember. He then has to play a round of the I- have-to-beat-the-checks-I-wrote-against-the-deposit game. Thankfully I only did that twice, and God protected us from enduring any penalties or jeopardizing our good credit rating.

All of us have forgotten things, but we must never forget to ask God what He would have us to do. Do not settle for just any old good plan. There is a risk that even though it is a good plan, it may fail. Walk in the most excellent way and ask God first. And guess what will happen? The Lord will tell you what His perfect plan is for you. He will guide your path. God loves us and is concerned about every area of our lives. Jesus was very clear about this when He said, "Seek ye first the kingdom of God and His righteousness, and all these things will be added unto you (Matthew 6:33).

The world would have us believe we can rebound from any mistake. We can go astray. We can forget things we know to do that are good and right. We can listen to the voices of those around us rather than the clear voice of God. It is true to some extent, that we can rebound from mistakes. God is forgiving and He is a redeemer and a restorer. He can help us in any situation in which we make mistakes; however, there are always consequences. For example, the law of gravity will work if you jump off a building. Likewise, if you jump in front of a fast-moving train, there is a strong possibility that train will hit you before it can slow down. Yes, God is able to save you; we know that He can perform miracles, but we must not put Him to a foolish test. We must never put ourselves in a position in which we are trying to force God to perform a miracle on our behalf.

God calls us to be wise as serpents but harmless as doves (Matthew

10:16). He calls us to seek His guidance first so that we do not have to pay the cost for our mistakes. We are to ask for wisdom from God on a daily basis. God desires us to ask Him for wisdom, and His Word says that He will give it liberally and not resent it. James 1:5-6 tells us that not only will God give us wisdom freely, but we must receive it without doubting Him. God wants us to be consistent and stable-minded, not wavering. We should expect that what God has said will come to pass.

Some mistakes really do cost more than others. Some mistakes may even cost us our relationship with God, which is the ultimate, unwanted price to pay. We must always seek God, follow God, and live God's way. Only then will we be able to live and operate in the real world.

STUDY AND DISCUSSION QUESTIONS –
CHAPTER NINE

1. Discuss a time when you decided something that you knew was totally in line with God's will for you.

2. How did you know that you were in line with Gods will?

3. Discuss a time when you moved ahead of God, maybe even outside of His will for you.

4. How did you know that you were not in line with God's will?

5. How do you know what God's wisdom looks like?

6. How can you explain wisdom to others?

7. Name someone in your life who you believe displays the wisdom of God.

8. Do you think that wisdom is the number one need in the body of Christ?

9. If so why? If not, why not?

10. Stop and pray for God's wisdom in every part of your life right now.

CHAPTER TEN

WALKING FORWARD
BUT LOOKING BACK

We all want to move forward. Forward with our careers, forward with our health, forward with our education, forward with our relationships. Looking back, or "living in the past" is often viewed in a negative way. When people do not see progress or forward movement they may become depressed, sad, and hopeless. Without growth, change, and forward movement, the human mind begins to suffer. Feeling stagnant can cause us to lose creativity, momentum, and energy.

Can you imagine walking or dancing while looking behind you? We would all think that was a little crazy. Our likely response would be, "I can't do that." We need to be able to see what's in front of us in order to know where we are going and plan our next steps; it's hard to find as much value in looking back. The front windshield is the largest window in your car for a reason. It is important to be able to see from various angles what is ahead of you. These windshields are also full of technology these days, like anti-glare lenses, built-in defrosters for fog and ice, no-glare technology, and state-of-the-art break resistant glass. The back window is usually smaller than the front window. Rearview and side mirrors in your car are there to:

1. Assure that you can see what is approaching you
2. See what you just passed
3. Assist you when you need to change lanes.

But, my friends beloved of the Father, there is a very good reason for you to look back.

We are in a fight. Satan is waging war on our homes, our schools, our relationships, our jobs, our marriages, finances, children, and even our churches. Fear, worry, anxiety, depression, and hopelessness are more prevalent now than during any other time in history. You may wish you could just skip through life singing "It's a sunny day and everything is going my way," but if you believe that you are in for a rude awakening. Amos 6:1 says, "Woe to you who are at ease in Zion."

Deuteronomy 20:1-4 discusses the strategic battle plan for war. The United States of America spends billions of dollars a year making sure that we are ready for war. The Department of Defense and other security agencies evaluate all possible enemies and threats to our national security. The government purchases weapons and equipment to stockpile for future use and ready key personnel with appropriate training to handle any threat. While all of this is good and necessary, God's plan for battle is simple. God has always used the simple to confound the wise. His battle strategy involves you remembering these three words:

JUST LOOK BACK.

When the enemy of our souls looks like he is going to overtake you, just look back. Don't be afraid when it looks like you are outnumbered or conquered; don't be frightened . . .just look back.

Just look back and:

Remember how God brought you through.

Remember how God raised you up when you were down.

Remember how God kept a roof over your head.

Remember how God healed you, body, mind, and soul.

Remember how God sustained you.

Remember how God never, ever left you.

There are times when it is important to look back, particularly when it comes to your faith in God. God often takes us through various stages of growth. We do not grow in our faith all at once; it is through experiences and victories that we are able to build up and stand on our faith. The Bible instructs us in James 1: 2-4, "My brethren, count it all joy when ye fall into diverse temptations. Knowing this, that the trying of your faith worketh patience. But let patience have her perfect work, that ye may be perfect and entire, wanting nothing." We are told to rejoice in tribulation because tribulations work patience, and patience works hope, hope works experience, and experience makes us unashamed. Experience with God helps us to learn how to trust Him during times of testing and tribulations. Because of this experience, we learn how to trust Him more and more. We learn how to navigate our way through existing trials and tribulations by reviewing our past experiences with God. We can "rewind the tape" and recall how the Lord brought us through. We can recall how He worked all things together for our good because we love Him and are called according to His purposes. Part of our success with God involves looking back to gather strength for the present and the future. There is a popular Christian song by Dawn Thomas and recorded by Shirley Caesar entitled, "He'll Do It Again." The chorus of the song states, "Hasn't He always come through for you? (. . .) You may not know how, and you may not know when, but He'll do it again" (Thomas, 1987).

Experience with God is extremely important. Your victory is behind you--the reminder that the same God who brought you through before has not changed. He is the Lord and He changeth not (Malachi 3:6). "Jesus Christ is the same yesterday, and today, and forevermore" (Hebrews 13:8). His love for you is still intact. His power is still great. It is the Lord who fights for you. The battle is the Lord's. Look back today and let God multiply your faith.

Live in the Real World going forward, but don't ever forget to reflect back on the faithfulness and blessings of God in your life.

STUDY AND DISCUSSION QUESTIONS – CHAPTER TEN

1. Take a piece of paper and a pen and write down three areas in which you have seen the Lord bring you through a victory. (It could be in the area of finances, health, job, relationships, safety, etc.)

What do you remember about these experiences?

2. If you cannot think of any area in which the Lord has assisted you and given you victory, write down three areas where you would like Him to give you victory.

3. If you could do something different, either in a previous trial or in a current trial, what would it be and why?

4. The Scriptures state that trials and tribulations work patience, hope, and experience into us. Write down how you obtained these three things in your situation.

5. Can you think of someone in your life who is "stuck in the past," which is different from looking back?

6. What sorts of things keep us from being able to move forward in God?

7. Ask the Lord to show you how to pray for and provide support for this person in you life who is stuck in the past.

CHAPTER ELEVEN

LOSING WEIGHT

"Run the race of faith . . . and leave behind those weights that so easily beset you" (Hebrews 12).

You may have immediately thought I would be talking about physical or body weight in this chapter. American culture is very weight-obsessed. We talk about it constantly. We spend millions on pills, powders, and potions that promise to reduce or refine our excess weight. We spend countless hours in the gym and exercising to impact our body weight and body mass. We make fashion choices based on body weight. We are denied some job opportunities because of weight. The food we eat is often chosen because of how it will impact our weight first, rather than its nutritional value. Most people do not want to tell others the actual number on the scale that represents their physical weight. We often dread going to the Doctor for a weigh-in because we are often disappointed with the results on the scale. I have family members who are upset because they feel they are too fat and I have family members who worry they are too skinny. It is amazing how much time American society spends thinking about weight.

Now don't get me wrong. I am definitely a proponent for health-- Healthy eating, healthy lifestyles, healthy exercise, healthy choices for recreation. I believe the Lord has called us to follow His model for wisdom and moderation in all things. I believe the Lord has made us stewards over the bodies He has given us, which we are to protect and care for. Caring for our bodies honors God, because our bodies are temples in which the Holy Spirit dwells. This is good and right to do, and is an important part of our reasonable service unto the Lord.

However, I am not talking about physical weight here. I am talking about weights that bother our souls and our spirits.

Emotional weights.

Spiritual weights.

Weights that keep us from *living in the real world* – the world in which Jesus is the only Lord.

Life is full of weights--challenges, burdens, obstacles, oppositions, frustrations, and problems. A weight is any person, place, or thing—any idea, memory, issue, or feeling--that causes us pain or keeps us from full peace and progress. Some weights in our lives are short-term occurrences, while others are more long term. Some weights are daily; some are weekly, monthly or intermittent. Some weights involve people--our family, friends, enemies, acquaintances, co-workers, neighbors, or even strangers. There are people in our lives who cause us much pain. Their presence, their conversation, and their interactions with us are sources of pain, not joy. They do not add peace to our lives, but rather a sense of heaviness. There are also places that can be a source of weight. Maybe something unpleasant happened to you in a particular city or town, and the mere thought of it becomes a burden to you. It could be a place of employment. Maybe it is a building, a neighborhood, or some location where you were harmed in some way. If you do not want to go back there, that place is probably a weight to you. Things—inanimate objects—may also be weights. Drugs and alcohol, which can induce unhealthy addictions, may have become weights to you. Weights take on all sorts of names: family, friends, co-workers, money, society, health, community, school, and in some instances, even church. Weights, weights, weights. Weights everywhere. We all have them. We all know them.

And none of us want them.

Yet they are there, constantly impacting us, weighing us down. Keeping us from flying freely. Keeping us from experiencing the full measure of freedom and peace we all long for and desire.

But there is always an answer for us in the word of God. Part of that answer is in the book of Hebrews. Many historians and bible scholars are not sure who wrote the book of Hebrews, though the writing is often attributed to the Apostle Paul. Irrespective of the author, many Bible experts guess that this book was written during a six-year window of opportunity - after the Emperor Nero started to persecute Christians in AD 64, but before AD 70. It was in AD 70 that the Romans tore down the Temple in Jerusalem. The people who lived during this time knew about persecution. They knew what it was like to carry many weights.

Remember, the Bible states there is nothing new under the sun. In other words, in today's vernacular: "The names have changed, but the story is still the same."

One very important lesson we see in the book of Hebrews is how to deal with weights. The book of Hebrews encourages us to throw off those weights that burden us.

Lose that weight.

Hebrews 12:1-3 states, "Wherefore, seeing we also are encompassed about with so great a cloud of witnesses, let us lay aside every weight, and the sin which doth so easily beset us, and let us run with patience the race that is set before us, Looking unto Jesus, the author and finisher of our faith; who for the joy that was set before Him endured the cross, despising the shame, and is set down at the right hand of the throne of God. For consider Him that endured such contradiction of sinners against Himself, lest ye be wearied and faint in your minds."

Jesus is our example of how to address weights.

Jesus is our model for how to deal with weights.

Jesus provides guidance on how to lay aside weights.

How do we do that? By fasting, prayer, faith, confessions, and service to others. These are all the things that our Lord and Savior Jesus Christ did during His ministry on earth, which helped Him remember that He was really *living in the real world* – in other words, a world where the Spirit of God is in charge, and not the flesh of men. Jesus modeled how it was possible to be in this world but not of it. He showed us that it is possible to live each and every day and make it count for the Kingdom of God. We know that we are not Jesus, but we also know that we must strive to walk as He walked and live as He lived. No matter what kind of weight we are carrying and no matter for how long, it is not impossible to lose weight. With the help and strength of the Lord to guide us, we can do it. With prayer, and faith in the Word of God, we can indeed lose any and all weights. If we will just begin by placing one foot in front of the other, we will see how the Lord will assist us in losing our weight. It will not always be an easy task. Some days may be easier than others. Sometimes the weight may fall off and other times the weight will come off after a battle. This is where our confessions can be powerful tools, because we know that the power of life and death are in the power of the tongue. We must make our confession--our conversation--line up with the knowledge that it is possible and probable that our weights are being removed. We have assuredness and confidence that weights can be lifted and destroyed from our lives. This confidence will give us the strength and ability to then go out and serve others who are also bearing weights.

Serving others is an acknowledgement that we trust and believe that God is caring, concerned, and practical. When others around us bear weights, we are often so blinded by the pressure of our own weights that we become apathetic, callous, critical, and challenged by the weights of others. This makes us not want to reach out to them to help them lift their weights. We become hardened and unconcerned about anyone else's weight but our own. This can make us reluctant to exert the energy, time, and resources to help others with their weights until we are free from our own. But it is then—even while burdened with our own weight--that we should and must serve others as Jesus served. There were times in the Holy Scriptures where Jesus was fatigued, hungry, aggravated, and saddened, but He never missed an opportunity to address the weights of others. This is our model. This is our example. I am a firm believer that you do indeed "reap what you sow." As you pour into the lives of others, the Lord will pour into your life. As you help others to set aside their weights, which are so easily besetting them, then I believe the Lord will help to set aside our weights. In this way, we all walk together as a faith community, trusting and believing God as we rejoice collectively in His answered prayers.

This is how we live lightly--free of weights--in the real world.

STUDY AND DISCUSSION QUESTIONS – CHAPTER ELEVEN

1. Name a time in your life where you were/are carrying weights.

2. Identify those specific weights in your life.

3. How did those weights become a part of your life?

4. What was your specific role in assisting those weights to encumber your life?

5. What changes have you made, if any, to relinquish the weights in your life?

6. Do you know others who are carrying weights?

7. Who are they and what are their weights?

8. What can you do to assist them?

9. Identify specifically how you can follow Jesus's model to remove the weights in your life.

10. Identify specifically how you can follow Jesus's model to help those identified in Question #6 to remove the weights in their life.

CHOOSING WHILE YOU
HAVE THE CHANCE

*L*ife is not always promised to you. You have 3 score and 10 days assigned – and then there is the sovereign hand of God. Salvation is not something you should put off until you feel like you have had all your worldly fun. It is not something you should do once you have cleaned yourself up. It is not something you should do after you have solved all your life problems. If you could solve all your own problems, you would not need salvation.

If you lose your health, your peace, or your privacy, your choices can change. Losing any of these things can have a significant impact on your life that may be irreversible. Your life can change in an instant. You may think all is well, and then with one event you will quickly realize that is not so.

You may believe you have things all figured out.

Planned out.

Measured out.

And then, POW!!! Life takes an immediate turn. One wrong decision in a car, one bad prescription medicine or over-the-counter drug, one bad medical procedure, one bad meal, one injury, can change the trajectory of your life. Your health could be so greatly impacted that this one event now takes you in a totally different direction. I once heard a wheelchair-bound man state that being disabled was the one club to which any and all could end up belonging, with or without choosing to be members. Your plans, no matter how sound, can be changed in an instant.

If you lose your peace, your life will also be altered. This could be connected to losing employment, losing a loved one, losing financial security, losing housing or food stability, or losing important relationships. Each of these has an impact on our peace.

In the global world of today, where security concerns us all, there is great regard for privacy. Millions of dollars and countless hours are spent trying to invade the privacy of individuals and organizations, and millions of dollars and countless hours are spent trying to protect the privacy of individuals and organizations. Entire enterprises and companies have been formed around the topic of privacy and security. There is a big difference between what is private and what is secret, but we know that release of either one can be damaging. I once heard my Pastor give an illustration about this topic. She asked the audience about the fact that all humans go to the bathroom. Is that true? All in the audience responded, "Yes." We all know that our bodies are made to perform two functions to allow the elimination of liquid and solid waste everyday--and if these functions do not happen, there is a life-threatening problem. My Pastor stated that all humans go to the bathroom and what happens in the bathroom is not a secret because all people do it; however, when we go in the bathroom, it should be private. This is why we close the door and keep others out while we are executing these bodily functions.

There is an important point here. We do not sit around waiting for threatening things to happen to us every day. We live our lives the best we know how and try to prepare for some possible challenges while realizing that it will be impossible to protect ourselves against everything. This is why it is important to accept salvation in Jesus Christ today.

Today.

You do not have foreknowledge of what tomorrow will bring, but with salvation through Jesus Christ you know for sure that it will bring you a life with the Holy Spirit of Jesus Christ as your daily guide. The Word of God has not made a secret of the key to fullness of life and joy. It is available for all to receive. The time and day to receive it is *now*.

When you understand the value of salvation through Jesus Christ, you will hold the key to abundant life. You will hold the key to joy. You will hold the key to success. You will hold the key to victory over every circumstance. You will hold on to an anchor through every storm life may bring.

The Bible calls David a man after God's own heart (1 Samuel 13:14). David also possessed the key to life. Keys signify ownership, access, control, relationship, and invitation. You have all of this when you own a key.

You have the ability to make decisions about the thing to which you have a key.

You have flexibility and power over the thing to which you have a key.

David possessed an important key, and that key was praise. He understood the power, freedom, and importance of praise. David was an expert "praise-er." He praised God so hard one time that his clothes began to come off. This embarrassed his wife. David praised God when he was happy and when he was sad. He praised God when he was up and he praised God when he was down. He praised God when things were going well and he praised God when things were not going well. He praised God when he was righteous and he praised God even when he had done wrong. He praised God when he experienced victory and he praised God when he experienced defeat.

I believe this key that David possessed allowed him to be called a man after God's own heart. This key allowed David to unlock the favor of God. It allowed him to tap into the heartbeat of God, to open up the favor and blessings of God. The key of praise opened up access to the Heavenlies. David had the attention of the throne-room of God when he praised.

We need our own keys to have ownership of and access to the important things in life. Accept salvation in Jesus Christ by confessing and believing that He is the Son of God. Confess your sins and ask for His forgiveness, and you can experience salvation and eternal life as discussed in Romans Chapter 8.

Operating and living in the real world is for those who realize they need to choose while they still have the chance.

STUDY AND DISCUSSION QUESTIONS –
CHAPTER TWELVE

1. What do you perceive are barriers to salvation?

2. What does it mean to you to be saved?

3. What are the benefits of salvation? What are the downfalls?

4. What is the difference between a church-goer or a "do-gooder" and someone who is saved?

5. How do you know you are saved?

6. Is salvation permanent or can it be lost?

7. Is salvation for today?

8. Do you believe there are levels of salvation, or are all that are saved the same?

9. Can we live successfully on earth without salvation through Jesus Christ?

10. What do you think about deathbed confessions of salvation? Are they valid?

CHAPTER THIRTEEN

EATING RIGHT

$\mathscr{E}$ating right has become a trillion dollar industry around the world. People are spending millions of dollars trying to figure out what it means to eat right. Some think it means to eat only like they ate in the Old Testament. Some think it means to eat only a vegetarian, vegan, or paleo diet. Some think eating right means only eating organic; others think eating right means eating everything you like. There are many schools of thought about how to eat right. One thread running through all these theories is that food is a critical component of our life. It is our lifeblood. Without food, we will not survive long. Another important thread running through all these theories is the theory that "we are what we eat." In other words, the food you eat has an important and direct impact on the condition of your mental, physical, and spiritual health. If we have enough food to sustain us on a daily basis and are happy about the foods we eat, we can usually expect to have "good health."

Now, I do realize that good health is not just connected to food alone. I understand that living a God-fearing life, getting sufficient rest, and exercise also contribute to good health.

Throughout the multitude of research out there is the understanding that fruit is an important component of whatever eating pattern you decide to adopt. Fruits are not just important--they are critical. Fruits contain many of the vitamins and minerals that are important to human life. Studies show that we should not just eat fruit, but we should eat it regularly. Some experts suggest multiple servings of fruit daily. Eating fruit every day will lead to good health. While other foods have value, you cannot survive on them alone; however, some believe that you can live on fruits alone.

Some of the important characteristics of fruit are:

Fruit is "living" food with active nutrients. Fruit can be consumed in its natural state (unlike meats and meat products which are the carcasses of dead animals).

Fruit helps maintain the internal cleanliness of the body by stimulating the elimination process (unlike meat, which sits in the digestive system for long periods because it is hard to digest).

Fruit protects us against illness and disease. It bolsters the body's immune system.

The fruit of the Holy Spirit does these exact same things.

The Spirit of God is living, vibrant, and active. The nutrients are not faded in any way. God is the same today as He was yesterday, and as He forever will continue to be (Hebrews 13:8). His power and His Word are alive and they will never fade away.

The fruit of the Spirit of God helps maintain cleanliness in our heart, body, and soul. It pushes out all the impurities of the world that bombard us on a daily basis. Just like fruits are chock-full of vitamins and minerals which help bolster the body against attack by disease by heightening the immune system, the Spirit of God protects us from the attacks of the world by preparing us--body, soul, and spirit. The Spirit of God bolsters us every day to be able to withstand the negative and harmful influences that would try to enter our hearts and minds.

There are analogies in the Word of God that I believe connect to real fruit.

Specifically, I believe there are:

Lemons of Longsuffering.
Peaches of Patience
Kiwis of Kindness
Star Fruit of Self Control

Grapes of Gentleness

Grapefruit of Goodness

Persimmons of Peace

Lemons of Longsuffering—_They're sour, but they're good for you._

Most of us can't eat them alone. But, when mixed with something else (water, tea, meat, soups, etc.), they provide a wonderful flavor. Lemons contain vitamin C, which helps bolster the immune system. The same is true of longsuffering. None of us really wants longsuffering and we definitely can't handle it alone. It has to be mixed with some courage, patience, and hope in order to give it a wonderful flavor. Longsuffering is important because it does increase our patience and our hope, which gives us a confidence in God that is unshakable.

I have walked through some trials in my life that left me feeling like my fruit of the Spirit was really getting a chance to grow. Not only did I feel it was growing, but I felt it was getting ripe and almost to the point of getting stinky. In fact, I felt like it was so overripe it was starting to get bugs in it. I personally felt like a fruit that had suffered so long I was going to soon fall from the tree and end up on the ground for the animals to devour. But, thanks be to God, who causes us to triumph in every circumstance and situation!

Peaches of Patience--*One large seed in the middle and lots of soft, sweet surrounding it.* You must eat this fruit with patience and caution, or you have the potential to damage your teeth as they come in contact with the hard seed in the middle. You must proceed with patience or what started out to be delightful can suddenly become dangerous. Such is it with life. We must proceed with patience in order to reap the full benefit of the beautiful life God wants for us. It is only when we forego patience that we rush and risk damage to ourselves, body, soul and spirit, because of our lack of patience.

Kiwis of Kindness – *Fuzzy and textured on the outside with a skin that must be peeled; soft, sweet, pulpy fruit on the inside.* Kindness unto others often requires us to peel away their fuzzy outsides to see their goodness on the inside. Kindness can be challenging because it can be viewed as weakness; however, exhibiting kindness to others allows us to receive the best of them, which is often hidden within a tough exterior. We must also learn to be kind with ourselves, realizing that we, too, are created in the image of God and therefore deserve good treatment.

Star Fruit of Self Control--*A star fruit is an interesting fruit with a tough and resilient outer peel that protects a soft and vulnerable inside.* If pressed too hard, the outside peel will bruise and become unsightly. This is true of us. We have this tough, outer shell, which is meant to protect our hearts. When we mistreat and disrespect ourselves by lacking self-control, we can damage our outside, which in turn leaves our inside vulnerable to attack. Unhealthy living, unhealthy lifestyles, and neglect of our bodies in any way can damage the "peeling" that was meant to protect our insides. Our emotions, hearts, and spiritual well-being are all impacted by the type of lifestyles we lead. Disobeying godly principles for living can have deadly consequences, especially if our hearts and minds are bruised due to lack of protection and covering. There is no way you can lack self-control and reap the fruit or benefits a disciplined, godly lifestyle enjoys.

Grapes of Gentleness--*Can be squeezed and bruised because both their skin and inside fruit are soft.* Although they possess a skin, grapes are tender and must be handled with gentle care. A grape can be squashed, making it unattractive or of little value. Grapes must be handled gently, just like we should handle our own lives. We should treat other people with the same gentle care we want others to exhibit with us. We should be gentle in our thoughts, words, and deeds. Gentleness helps to give us a certain measure of sweetness. You have to handle with care. Those who exhibit gentleness are sought after in this world in which so much is hard and bitter.

Grapefruit of Goodness – *Lots of seeds, but those who are willing to navigate the seeds are rewarded with the delicious and healthy fruit that lies intertwined.* Grapefruit can be a great source of Vitamin

C, which we can also get from being in the sun. When we live a life of goodness to others we are letting others know that we have been with the *Son* of God. God helps refine and define our character so that we will display His goodness in our thoughts, words and deeds.

Persimmons of Peace--*the large, orange, several-seeded fruit of the persimmon tree.* After being ripened, it provides a delicious fruit; it is, however, not desirable when not ripe. Peace is wholeness--a state of completeness that brings comfort, security, and true joy. Such is our peace with God. When He is in us and we are in Him, we can truly experience His perfect peace. This does not happen overnight. We must be tried, tested and found faithful to experience Gods full peace, and it is only through Him that peace is found.

Be full of the fruit of the Spirit so that you may be strong in every way and successfully live in the real world.

STUDY AND DISCUSSION QUESTIONS – CHAPTER THIRTEEN

1. Use a fruit to describe yourself and your walk with God.

2. Which fruit of the Spirit is the strongest or most prevalent in you?

3. Which fruit of the Spirit is the weakest in you?

4. Do you believe there is one fruit of the Spirit that is more important than the others?

5. If so, which one is it and why?

6. Write down a prayer thanking the Lord for helping you understand the significance of the fruit of His Spirit and for helping you exhibit it in your own life.

7. Describe someone you know who is a bad example of the fruit of the Spirit. Give specific examples about why.

8. Describe someone you know who is a good example of the fruit of the Spirit. Give specific examples about why.

9. What do you believe is the best way to develop the fruit of the Spirit?

10. Pray for yourself and those around you to live in the fruit of the Spirit daily.

CHAPTER FOURTEEN

YOU CAN'T COME OVER UNTIL YOU OVERCOME

*I*n this world you will face many enemies. Some enemies you may see, and other enemies you do not see. There are enemies you may know about, and there are enemies of which you are totally unaware. Some enemies are relatively benign in that they may not like you for some reason, but simply nurture their dislike from afar. Still others will expend their energy and resources to systematically set traps and plots against you.

I once had a supervisor who was so incredibly nasty on a daily basis that I began to question whether I was imagining it. Surely no one person could be so nasty, so regularly. It did not take me long to realize that this was just an "old fashioned satanic attack" and that it was nothing the Word of God could not handle. I understood that my supervisor's actions were wrong, but I needed to treat him the way Scripture says we should treat an enemy.

You know, *love those who use and hurt us.*

You know, *forgive those who mistreat us.*

You know, *pray for their well being despite their actions.*

You know, *offer them a drink of water if they are thirsty . . . walk the second mile. . . turn the other cheek . . . offer your coat as well as your cloak . . .*

I realized that my supervisor would not be the one to turn the Word of God into a lie. I realized he would not be the one to make God's Word of no effect. I realized that he would not be the one to overturn the

Word and the promises of God. I needed to respond like God's Word instructed me to respond, and I would see results in this situation.

I would see the victory in this situation.

I would be able to overcome, but I would have to do it God's way and not my own.

This supervisor's continued misogyny, racial attacks, and harassment drove me back to the practice of early morning prayer. I had previously started a practice of prayer, but I was beginning to reduce my time and intensity in prayer in the mornings. I was inconsistent. I was unfocused. My morning prayer time had turned into a quick rundown of the day's activities and a request for God to bless me during those activities. I had strayed away from a time of praise, worship, and adoration. I had strayed away from the time of thanksgiving I would spend before the Lord. But when you encounter an enemy like I had, you have to fight back using the weapons of our warfare, which are not carnal, but which are mighty through God for the pulling down of strongholds (2 Corinthians 10:4).

Although I had an attacker on my job, there are many accounts in the Holy Scriptures in which people were not just attacked, but also killed. One such account is the story of Saul's conversion to Paul. Saul was like a crazed madman when it came to hunting, torturing, and killing the Christians. He petitioned to get a court order that would allow him to search for Christians, chain them, and bring them back for trial. Acts 8:3 states, "As for Saul, he made havoc of the church, entering into every house and, hailing men and women, committed them to prison." Saul was even responsible for the stoning death of Stephen, serving as an accessory to the crime and holding the coats of those who actually did the stoning (Acts 8:1). Saul had to come out of his hatred, His ignorance, and his own self-focus in order to ultimately become an overcomer himself. Saul was destined for greatness, but God had to strip Him of his worldly, carnal worldview in order to help him become an example of overcoming—and God marked these changes by giving him a new name—Paul. Paul would ultimately suffer many things for the sake of the Gospel but he could not ultimately do his life's work until he came out of some things first.

There are times when mistreatment, harassment, and the work of an enemy will actually take you into the fulfillment of your purpose. Saul's mistreatment of Stephen ultimately helped Stephen fulfill his calling to be a martyr for the sake of the Gospel. It also helped transform Saul into Paul. Paul became an overcomer.

But it was not until he learned first to *come over* some things himself.

Paul's journey is actually quite fascinating, in that he had to come over his own shortcomings, and in doing so he opened the door to become an overcomer himself. Paul went through some very trying experiences--being shipwrecked, being bitten by a snake, being thrown in jail, being beaten, being betrayed, and eventually enduring endless in-fighting among the churches. Through all of this, Paul showed us what it meant to be an overcomer in every situation. He showed us that it is not how we start that counts; it is how we finish that ultimately counts. His start was rocky and shaky. But his finish was powerful and memorable.

We too may have to come over some things before we can be overcomers. We may have to come over our own shortcomings, but if we will continue to walk with God, we will be overcomers.

We may have to come over our own mistakes, but if we will continue to walk with God, we will be overcomers.

We may have to come over our own guilt and shame about things in our past, but if we will continue to walk with God, we will be overcomers.

We are not fully able to come over into God's joy, His peace, and His power until we overcome the world. Jesus was our example. He told us, in spite of tribulations, to be of good cheer--for He had overcome the world (John 16:33).

Because Jesus did it, we can too.

This is how we become able to truly operate and live in the real world.

6. Recall a situation where you witnessed firsthand someone overcoming something.

7. How did you see them overcome? What did they do?

8. Write a list of things you think are important components of becoming an overcomer.

9. Write a prayer thanking God for the strength, courage, and faith to become an overcomer in all the situations you face.

10. Pray for those around you to live as overcomers, as well as for yourself.

CHAPTER FIFTEEN

DON'T BE THE SAME FOOL TWICE

*I*f you are reading this book, you have probably been on this earth for more than a day. Anyone who has been on this earth for more than a day has had at least one opportunity to be offended and/or betrayed. Betrayal is a deadly weapon the enemy uses against us because the effects can be long lasting.

When you punch someone with your fist they may feel immediate pain, but unless you are a prizefighter, the sting and bruise from the punch will eventually go away. However, if that same person takes a knife and stabs you with it, the impact will go deeper; the blade could even penetrate vulnerable parts of the body, and the effects from the damage of a stabbing could last for many years to come. A betrayal by a friend or someone you loved or trusted is especially deadly. There are some betrayals that we are convinced we will never be able to overcome.

We believe we cannot overcome these wounds, in part, because we couple the physical pain from a betrayal with the emotional pain it leaves behind. When I have faced betrayals in my life, I have experienced some progressive and compounding emotions.

First, I had to get over the initial shock.

After getting over the initial shock, I began to wrestle with my own shortcomings:

Why was I so naïve that I did not see this coming?

Why did I not protect myself better in the first place?

Why did I not see that my betrayer was not worthy of my trust?

Why was I a fool for opening up to them and believing in their words, their actions, their smile?

After wrestling with my own shortcomings, I began to feel uncertian about the future:

What would make them do such a thing and why did I miss the signals?

Can I ever trust them again?

Should I ever trust anyone again?

All these feelings, and more, accompany a betrayal. This is why the enemy makes it his job to ensure that we all feel the sting of betrayal at some point in our lives. Some people feel the pain of betrayal as young children, when the adults assigned to care for, love, and train them fail in their responsibilities. These failures can establish a root of pain at an early age that may take a lifetime to overcome. As this root of pain grows, it can become a full-blown weed, often choking out the space and opportunity for other healthy plants to take root. This weed is often fed by additional disappointment, rejection, and betrayal, which is heaped on top of the initial one we experienced in our childhood.

Some people have experienced betrayal in adolescence. This can be particularly damaging because it is during adolescence that character is established, value systems are formed, sexuality is developing, and worldview is shaped. A betrayal during this season of life can have an impact on the direction a person's life will ultimately take. Studies have shown that betrayal by peers and trusted adults may even result in suicide among teenagers (Edwards, Freyd, Dube, Anda, and Felitti, 2012). Victims are so devastated by the betrayal that they often see no hope to ever overcome it, and begin to believe that life has no hope or possibility beyond this betrayal. They often feel broken and shattered. The skills to fully cope with life's setbacks have not yet been fully developed in adolescents, which may lead them down this path of no return.

As adults, we, too, face betrayals. I have experienced many betrayals in my lifetime, as I am sure you have as well. I remember one particularly painful betrayal that broke my heart into a thousand pieces. I was so devastated and shattered I was not sure I could ever really be whole again. I felt like a fool--a failure. I went through a full range of emotions including anger, disappointment, frustration, fear, and even physical pain. A betrayal of this depth is often accompanied by a visceral reaction. For several days I had a pain in my gut that just would not subside. I woke up with it; I fell asleep with it. I would wake up in the morning crying about it. I continued to re-live it, replaying it over and over. I was just so very, very hurt. I was angry that I had ever trusted my betrayer and I was angry that they would ever do such a thing to me. Some moments, I actually wanted to lay my "salvation in Jesus Christ" down for just a minute and physically harm them in some way, just to show them a measure of the pain they had caused me. I was disappointed because I had gauged them to be of better character than I eventually learned they were. I was fearful because I knew God would ultimately call me to forgive them, yet I honestly did not want to do that and I was not even sure that it could be done.

I felt like a fool.

I really felt like a fool.

I felt this way, primarily because I simply did not know how to deal with the initial and ongoing pain that is symptomatic of betrayal. And then I finally cried out to the Lord to help me. I cried out both literally and figuratively. God is so awesome, because He deals with us so very gently when we are in this state.

One of the first things the Lord did was remind me of a time a family member had suffered a broken bone. The bone was broken suddenly as a result of an accident. The break was quite extensive. This family member was in severe pain and even fell into self-blame for not being smart enough to avoid the accident. However, after weeks of medical treatments and therapies, the bone not only mended, but actually came back stronger than it was before the break.

The Lord reminded me that it is possible for a broken bone to mend and grow back even stronger than it was before. When you break a bone, your body is programmed to begin a process that will "knit" the bone back together and heal. Bone is a living tissue, just like your ligaments, heart, brain, and liver. When you break a bone, it is not like breaking a stick of wood; an injured bone will bleed, immediately beginning the healing process.

Technically speaking, a fracture triggers a process in which cells in your bone change from a resting state and become very active in regenerating new bone. This process produces what is called "fracture callus." When your doctor shows you the x-ray of a healing fracture, it will look like a big 'lump' of bone where the injury occurred. Sometimes during the healing process, you can actually feel this lump, which is normal. Once the ends of the bone have knitted themselves together, the body will then begin a process of remodeling the fracture callus. In many cases, the bone will eventually return to its normal appearance and it may even be difficult to tell there was ever a fracture.

Is the bone stronger after it has been broken?

This is a tricky question. In general, we don't go out and try to re-break a healed bone to see how strong it actually has become! Additionally, there is a time immediately after the final cast is removed when a bone is probably weaker than it was before the break. This is a time when you may want to try to limit more dangerous activities. However, when the bone is completely healed, the diameter of the bone is often bigger; it in this instance that the bone is actually stronger until it completely remolds back to its normal, pre-fracture state.

Much like bones can be broken, our hearts can also be broken. The Lord reminded me that there is no human being that is perfect. All the perfect(ed) people are already in His presence in heaven. In other words, all those who are perfect became that way because they left this earth. There was only one who walked the earth in perfection and that was Jesus Christ. We are all prone and susceptible to make mistakes, errors in judgment, act out of our own selfishness, and allow ourselves to become tempted by the devil's many tricks and deceptions. We must understand that we are not perfect and that we most likely have inflicted pain on those around us.

Therefore we must not be foolish in allowing others to hurt us--but we also must be careful not to hurt others. Let us learn to forgive quickly and completely. This way we will not let offense and bitterness take root in us by failing to recognize the works of the enemy. We may be impacted by hurt and betrayal in our lives but we must be careful to recognize Satan's devices that break us and take us away from the powerful, faith-filled life God has called us to enjoy. You may have been hurt once. You may still be hurting now.

But in the midst of your pain, don't be the same fool twice and let the works of Satan derail you from operating and living in the real world.

STUDY AND DISCUSSION QUESTIONS –
CHAPTER FIFTEEN

1.   Think of a time when you felt betrayed.

2. What were your initial feelings about it?

3. What were your secondary thoughts and feelings about it?

4. What did you decide to do about it?

5. How did that work out?

6. Were you able to maintain contact with the person who betrayed you?

7. If so, how, and if not, why not?

8. What do you think is the key to dealing successfully with betrayal?

9. Pray for those who have betrayed you.

10. Pray for yourself, that you will be able to forgive and learn to live in that power of forgiveness.

Chapter Sixteen

RECEIVING THE BREATH OF GOD

*W*hat is the breath of God? In order to answer this question, we need to know what breath is. Webster's Dictionary defines "breath" as "air inhaled and exhaled through breathing;" and it defines "breathe" as the ability "to exhale and inhale freely" (Merriam-Webster.com, 2017).

I believe the breath of any being is its life source, its essence, its power. It is the evidence of life's existence. It is the breath that constantly reminds the being that life is there. Breath is without break; when breath stops, there is no longer life. When breath is impeded or compromised in some way, life is impacted. Every living thing shares the act of breathing. Even plants have their own form of "breathing."

Breath often accompanies the beating of the heart. When the heart is functioning properly it is the breath that provides the required nourishment to keep the heart beating. The breath facilitates the blood to carry the nutrients/chemicals necessary for a heart to function. While there are other components to having a healthy heart (i.e. regular exercise, proper diet, and adequate rest), but without the act of breathing, none of these other things matter. Although they all impact the heart, nothing has the ability to stop the heart like lack of breath. When breath stops, the heart stops shortly after. A person can be pronounced medically brain dead and yet alive because there is breath. A body in which a brain ceases to function properly may still stay alive if there is breath. That breath may have to be assisted by medical equipment, medication, and electricity, but it is still there, and thus, there is still life.

When we accept the Lord Jesus Christ as our Savior we receive the breath of God. Yes, we know that God gives breath to every living being, but we do not receive *His* breath until we accept Jesus Christ and receive His salvation. Then God becomes our life force and our nourishment. He becomes the essence within us that allows us to really live each day. Yes, we had a natural life prior to salvation, but until we receive the breath of God we do not have spiritual life. The knowledge of God is not fully developed until we receive His breath. The ability to read and understand the Holy Bible is not developed until we receive the breath of God. In fact, the Scriptures tell us that the things of God are like foolishness to those who have not received His Holy Spirit (1 Corinthians 2:14).

I believe God desires to breathe His breath on us all. He wants us to receive His essence, His lifeblood, His being.

He wants us to sense His presence throughout our entire day.

He wants us to depend on Him.

He wants us to know that He is there, sustaining us, supporting us, and maintaining us.

Without Him, our hearts cannot properly function.

We may find ourselves in situations in which our brain has gone dead, so to speak. We do not know who we are, what to do, where to go, or how to live. We may be hurt and disappointed. We may feel confused or angry. We may have been abused or betrayed. We may feel jealous. We may be exhibiting any number of human emotions, rendering us without full "brain power." But the good news is that as long as there is breath, we are able to live on. God is able to take every situation and turn it around for our good. Romans 8:28 reminds us, "And we know that all things work together for good to them that love God and are the called according to the will of God."

He is the breath that sustains us. He is the breath that is there to constantly remind us we are indeed alive. He is the breath that supplies all the nutrients and other components necessary for our hearts to keep beating.

As long as there is breath, there is hope.

As long as there is hope, there is help.

With hope and help, life's circumstances can be turned around. Life's challenges can be faced. Life's obstacles can be overcome. Life's disappointments can be reversed. Life's dry places can become watered.

It is the breath of God that reminds us that He is in control. Have you ever tried to hold your breath? I remember playing a popular game when I was a child, the object of which was to see who could hold their breath the longest. Well, as you can imagine and probably know from playing this game yourself, it was quite difficult and totally impossible to hold our breath but for so long. Inevitably, we each would have to take a breath, despite our attempts to not do so. These attempts would often result in us sputtering and spitting as we failed to hold our breath any longer.

This was a child's game, but we sometimes play this game as adults, don't we?

We try to do things on our own.

We try to solve our own problems.

We try to control our life's functions.

Only to find out we ultimately must depend on God's breath to sustain us.

We cannot live in the real world without living and depending on the very breath of God. It is in Him that we live, and move, and have our being (Acts 17:28). The breath of God is our constant reminder that He is there to uphold us and keep us alive. Just like our natural breath and the breathing process is paramount to natural life, so the breath of God is paramount to spiritual life.

It is the breath of God that ultimately allows us to live and operate in the real world.

STUDY AND DISCUSSION QUESTIONS - CHAPTER SIXTEEN

1. What does the breath of God mean to you?

2. Describe a time when you tried to make something happen on your own without God.

3. Describe a time when you knew the Lord had breathed life into your situation.

4. How did you know specifically that the Lord had breathed on you and your situation?

5. Describe some things that can impede your breath in the natural realm.

6. Describe some things that can impede your breath in the spiritual realm.

7. Discuss a time when you tried to "hold your breath."

8. What finally made you breathe again?

9. Have you ever had someone else try to impede your breathing? How did you break free?

10. Have you ever tried to impede someone else's breathing? How did they break free?

Chapter Seventeen

LAYING DOWN SO YOU CAN RISE UP

*E*veryone wants to be *on top*. This is a common goal in America. We want to be on top and we want to live on top. There are even popular songs that reference "putting my love on top" (Beyonce, 2011), or "standing on the top" (James, 1982). The concept of being on *the top* indicates we are above everything and everyone else around.

There is no one and nothing above us.

We are over everyone and everything.

Everything else is under our feet because we are on the top.

We are in the superior position--the position of exaltation.

Everyone and everything else has to look up to us because we are the ones on top.

This is the place everyone wants to be. I have never heard of anyone with proper self-esteem who makes it his or her goal to be on the bottom, or who desires to be beneath everyone and everything else. Now, we all know that life's circumstances can certainly take us there, or at least make us feel like we are there already. But even if we find ourselves on the bottom, we always attempt to get back to the top. We keep working, we keep strategizing, we keep trying to manage the outcome and make our way back to the top.

This is why we must learn how to live and operate in the real world. In the spiritual world, it was Jesus Christ who was our role model for servanthood. He was our example of someone who laid down do that He could rise up. He laid down His life, His position, and His glory so

He could rise up--and so *we* could rise up, as well. He was willing to give up His benefits so He could show us true love and servanthood. He went to the cross and gave His life so that we could be reconciled back to the Father. No man took Jesus' life; He willingly laid it down for each and every one of us.

Philippians 2: 3-7 tells us:

> Let this mind be in you, which was also in Christ Jesus: Who, being in the form of God, thought it not robbery to be equal with God: But made Himself of no reputation, and took upon Him the form of a servant, and was made in the likeness of men: And being found in fashion as a man, He humbled Himself, and became obedient unto death, even the death of the cross. Wherefore God also hath highly exalted Him, and given Him a name which is above every name: That at the name of Jesus every knee should bow, of things in heaven, and things in earth, and things

under the earth; And that every tongue should confess that Jesus Christ is Lord, to the glory of God the Father.

Jesus Christ our Savior laid down His comfort and His position and humbled Himself, even unto death, so that He could rise up after the crucifixion. When He rose up, He had all power in His hands! By rising from the dead Himself, He gave us the power to rise with Him.

The only way to rise up in the real world is to follow Jesus' example and lay some things down.

Lay down your pride.

Lay down your status.

Lay down your accomplishments and serve the Kingdom of God so that you, too, can rise up.

Learn how God's words and His ways are the only things that are real in this world. By following Him entirely, we can truly learn how to successfully live and operate in the real world.

STUDY AND DISCUSSION QUESTIONS - CHAPTER SEVENTEEN

1. Describe a time or situation when you felt you were on top.

2. Describe a time or situation when you felt you were not on top.

3. How did you specifically know when you were or were not on top?

4. How do you feel when you see others on top?

5. Describe a situation when you had to step aside and let someone else get to the top?

6. How do you think that person(s) perceived your actions?

7. Describe ways that you think Jesus Christ was on top.

8. Describe ways that you think Jesus Christ was not on the top.

9. Describe some others in the Bible who laid down their lives so that they could rise up.

10. What will you do to serve the Kingdom of God, now and in the future?

References

James, Rick. Standing on the Top. *Reunion.* Recorded by The Temptations featuring Rick James, Motown/Sony/RCA records, 1982, New York, NY.

Knowles, Beyonce, Shae Taylor, and Nash Terius. Love on Top. *4.* Sony/ATV Music Publishing LLC, Warner/Chappell Music, Inc., Downtown Music Publishing LLC

Mehl, M. R., Vazire, S., Ramírez-Esparza, N., Slatcher, R. B., & Pennebaker, J. W.(2007). *Are women really more talkative than men?* Science, 317, 82.

Merriam-Webster, *Webster's Revised Unabridged Dictionary.* C. and G. Merriam Company, Springfield, Mass: Merriam-Webster Inc., 1913

Merriam-Webster, *New College Edition*. C. and G. Merriam Company, Springfield, Mass.: Merriam-Webster Inc., 1983. [9th ed.]

Merriam-Webster.com. Merriam-Webster, 2017. Web. 27 August 2017

Swaminathan, Nikhil, *Gender Jabber: Do Women Talk More Than Men?* Scientific American, July 6, 2007

Thomas, D. (1987). He'll Do It Again. Recorded by Shirley Caesar, *I Remember Mama,* 1989. Retrieved from www.constan-tchangemusic.com

About the Author

*M*rs. Julie Taitt was born in St. Louis, Missouri. She relocated to the Washington, D.C. area and graduated from T.C. Williams High School. Julie continued her education and earned a Bachelor's degree in Biology with a minor in Business Administration and a Master's degree in Education. She is currently working on her doctoral degree.

Julie was employed by the U.S. Federal Government for over 30 years prior to her retirement. While in the Government, Julie served in various aspects of senior management, leadership and supervision. Julie also served as a trainer for the Government, teaching classes to agency supervisors and leaders.

Julie is the Founder and President of J. Taitt and Associates, LLC. Her company is both a Prime and Subcontractor to many organizations and federal agencies throughout the United States, performing curriculum development and providing consulting services on team building and leadership.

Julie has been married for over 33 years and is the mother of two adult children. She and her family are world travelers who enjoy immersing themselves in the local culture. Julie is an avid reader and loves music. She is very involved in ministry through her church where she runs a mentoring program for girls. Julie also participates in worldwide missionary trips to aid the hungry, foster education, and alleviate suffering.

It was Julie's love for reading and ministry that compelled her to express herself through writing. She believes the written word lives forever and has the power to transform our lives. It is her belief that God loves us all and has given us all wisdom so that we can prosper and succeed in the real world. This writing reflects God's wisdom and is sure to impact you.

People have a tendency to live by their senses. We focus on what we see, hear, and feel. While this is ok, it is not all we are called to rely on. As we all know, it is quite possible to be deceived by what we think we see—and by what we think we hear. There are times when we may later realize that our initial assessments were not at all true; our eyes may have deceived us. Our ears may have deceived us. So what is real?

The only thing that is real is the Holy Bible and the wisdom from God contained in it.

It is my prayer that this book, Living in the Real World, will inspire you, encourage you, enrich you as you too learn how to daily live in the real world.

For speaking engagements, group book signings, retreats, workshops, seminars, or training sessions, please contact the Author at:

wisdomfortherealworld.com

Acknowledgements

I want to give thanks first and foremost to God, in whom I live and move and have my being.

A special Thank You to all my friends, family, and colleagues for helping me, believing in me, and praying for me as I fulfilled the task of this published book.

Truly only the LORD can repay you.

CPSIA information can be obtained
at www.ICGtesting.com
Printed in the USA
LVHW02s0359290318
571534LV00002B/25/P